# WESTERN DESERT SUBLIME

## The Craig Edwards Gift to the ANU

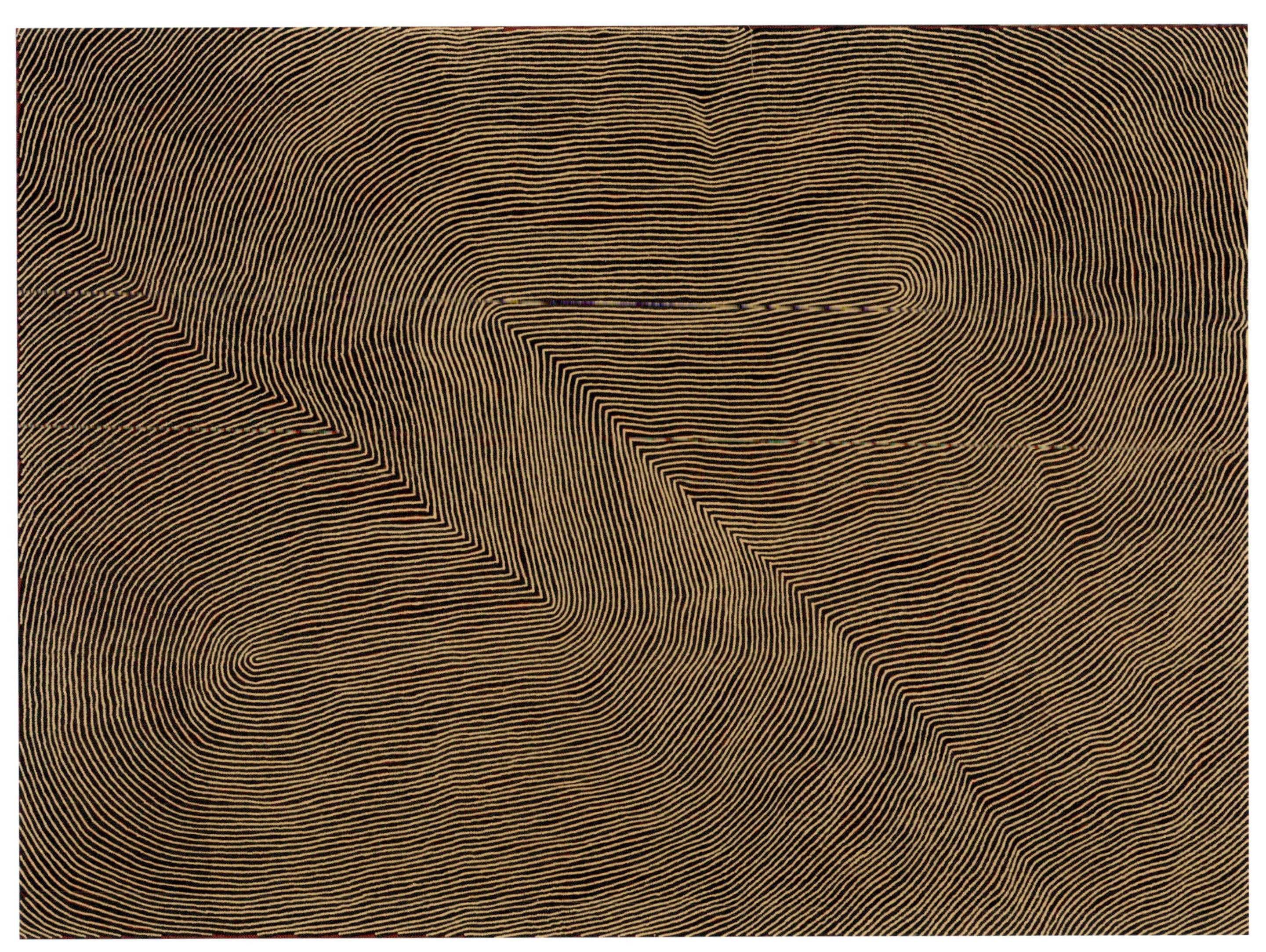

Warlimpirrnga Tjapaltjarri, *Untitled* 2008, acrylic on canvas, 183 x 244 cm
overleaf: Lorna Napanangka, *Untitled* 2009, acrylic on canvas, 244 x 485 cm

# Contents

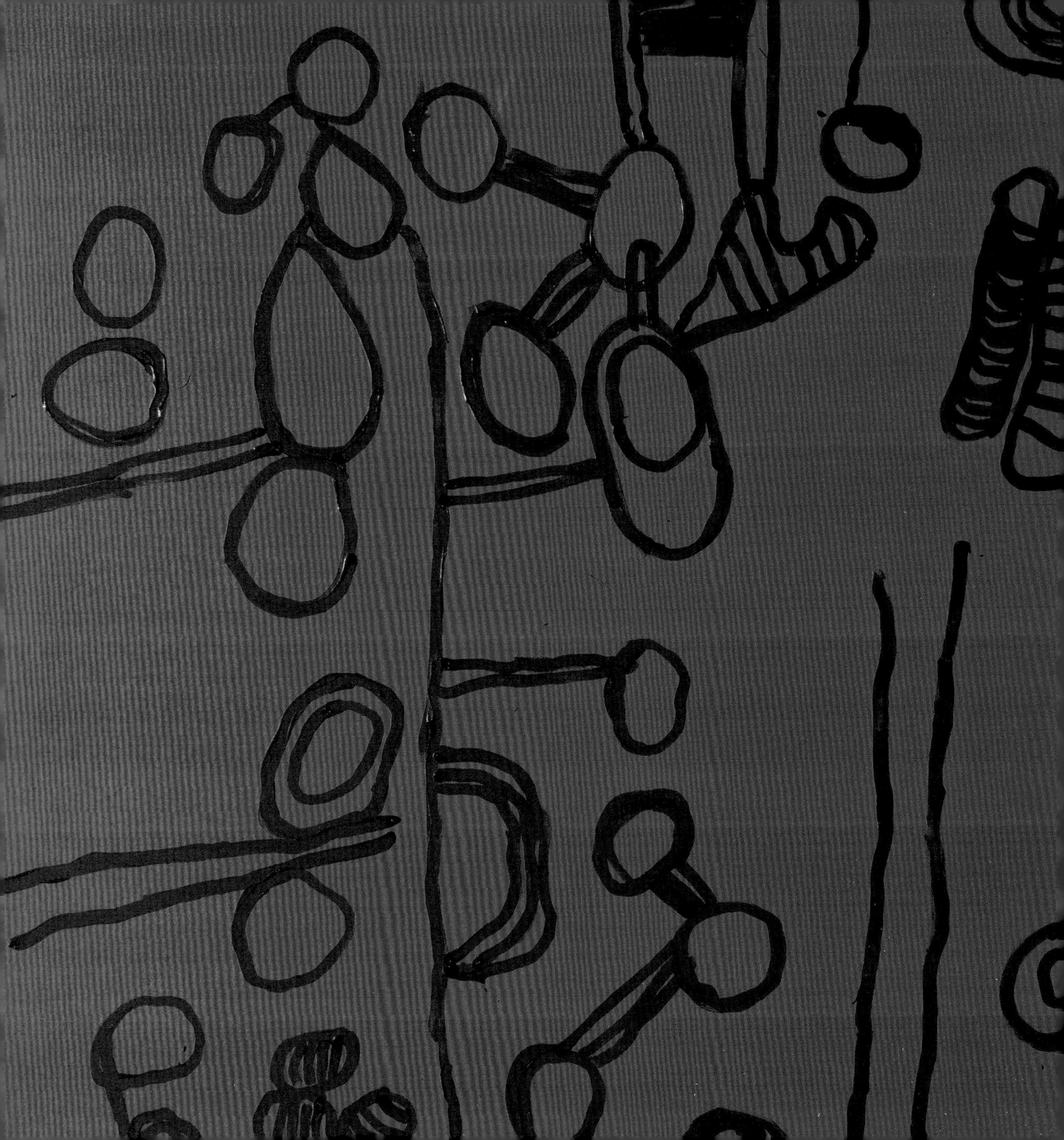

Queenie McKenzie

Yinarupa Gibson Nangala

Esther Giles Nampitjinpa

Kayi Kayi Nampitjinpa (Barbara Reid Napangarti)

Nyurapayia Nampitjinpa (Mrs Bennett)

Tjawina Porter Nampitjinpa

Linda Syddick Napaltjarri

Lorna Napanangka

Dorothy Napangardi

Nyungawarra Ward Napurrula

Ningura Napurrula

Jorna Newberry

Mel Yamba Nungurrayi

Naata Nungurrayi

Nancy Ross Nungurrayi

Tiger Palpatja

Ray James Tjangala

Warlimpirrnga Tjapaltjarri

Pinta Pinta Tjapanangka

Wimmitji Tjapangati

George Tjungurrayi

Yannima Pikarli Tommy Watson

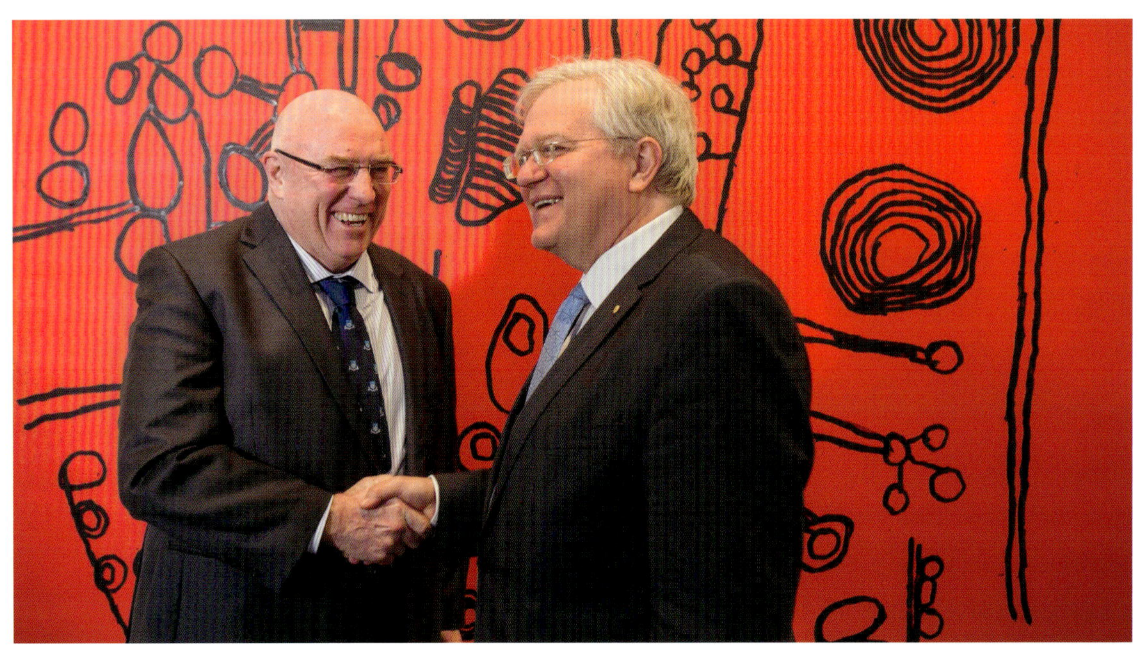

Craig Edwards and Professor Brian Schmidt with painting by Naata Nungurrayi, *Iconography* 2008

## Vice Chancellor's Foreword

This landmark gift of art given by Craig Edwards to ANU is the most valuable donation of its kind ever received by an Australian university. It comprises 120 paintings valued at over nine million dollars, an incredibly rich and enduring resource for the Canberra community as well as future generations of students, staff and visitors to ANU.

Since my commencement as Vice-Chancellor in early 2016, I have been determined that ANU will play a leadership role in promoting the reconciliation of our First Nations people. It is my wish that the University seize every available opportunity to learn from Aboriginal and Torres Strait Islander peoples. We have taken some important steps towards that goal already. Recently, at our First Nations Forum, the University hosted an open discussion among local and international Indigenous peoples in regard to actions and events of reconciliation we hope will take place in Australia.

Consequently we are delighted Craig has chosen ANU and the Drill Hall Gallery to be the beneficiaries of his art collection and of the legacy of the artists who are featured in it.

Craig began collecting Indigenous art in 1994 and has shaped a collection unique in character and scope. It highlights some of the outstanding female artists of the Western Desert who emerged into public view over the past two decades, and represents them through some of their strongest, most ambitious works.

Over recent years Craig has supported the ANU Drill Hall Gallery with personal donations and ongoing sponsorship through his law firm Maliganis Edwards Johnson. Now he gives an unprecedented boost to the University's art collection whose exponential growth has occurred largely because of the generosity of donors, testifying to the culture of philanthropy that is growing among alumni and friends of ANU.

Every time we observe the beauty and resilience of Indigenous art, we are reminded of the unique power of its connection to Country.

These paintings will make a huge contribution in defining the whole tenor of the University environment. It is a historic and momentous gift and we thank ANU alumnus and close friend, Craig Edwards, for his generosity, leadership and vision.

Professor Brian P. Schmidt AC FAA FRS

Vice-Chancellor,
Australian National University

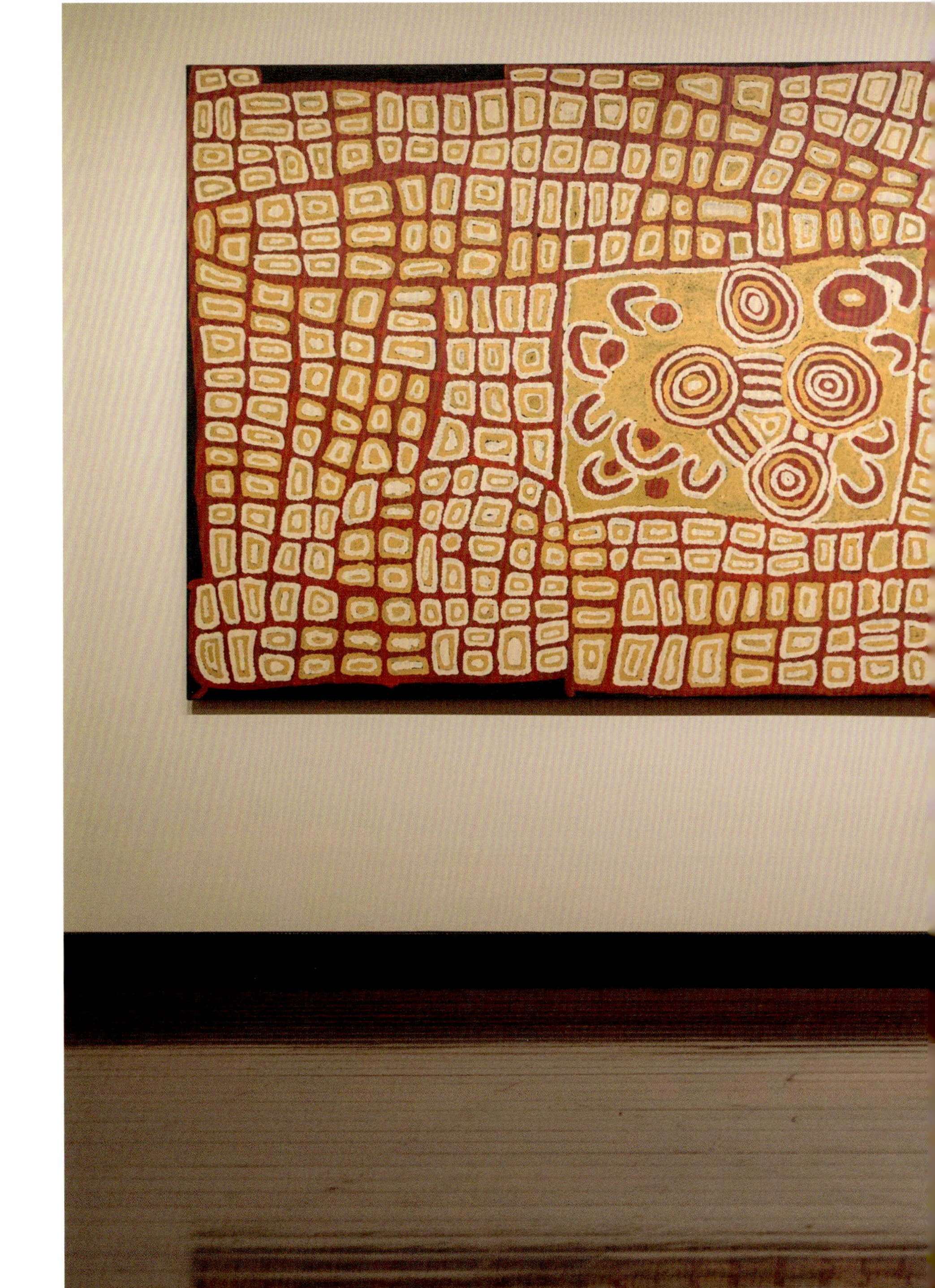

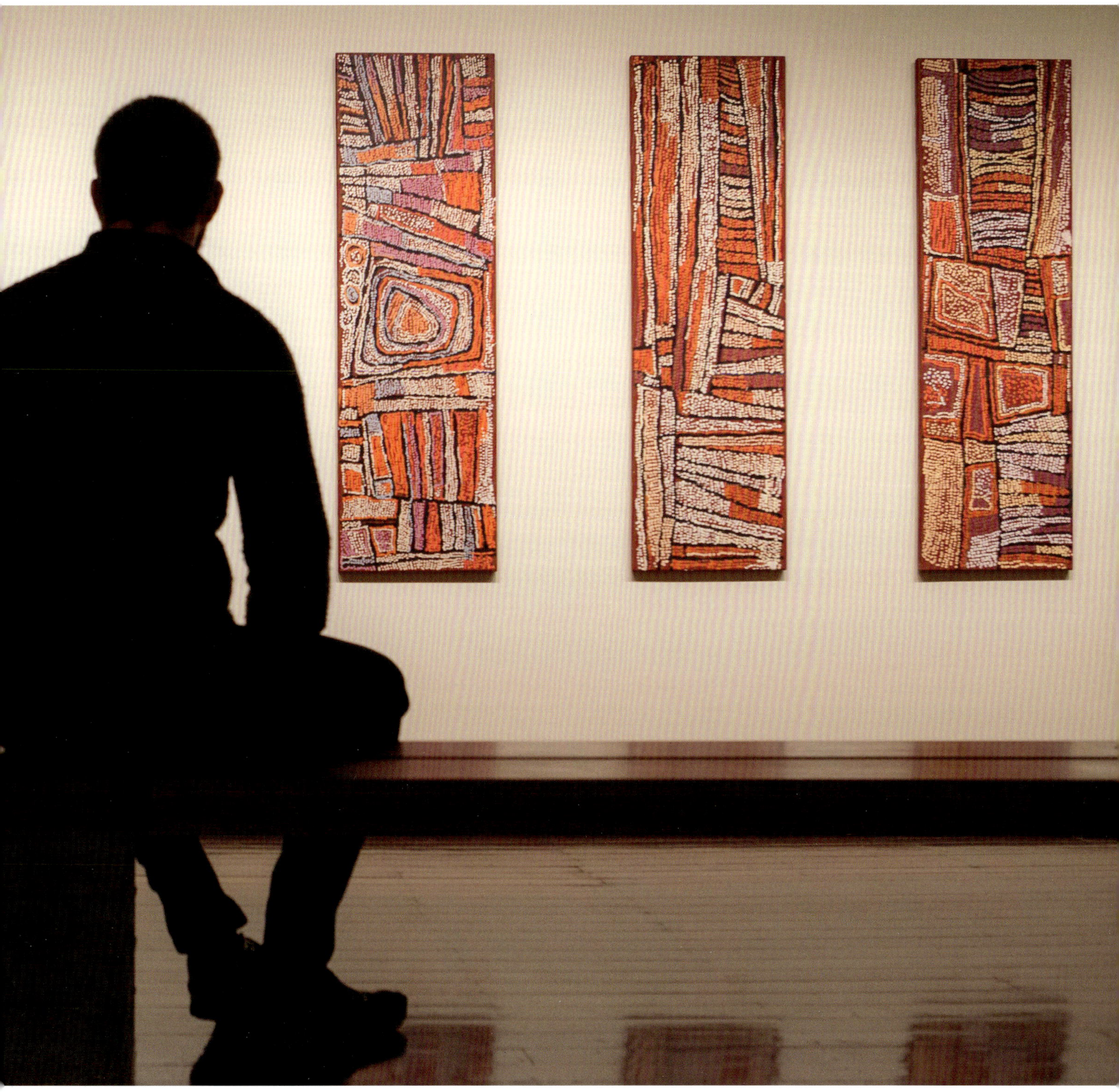

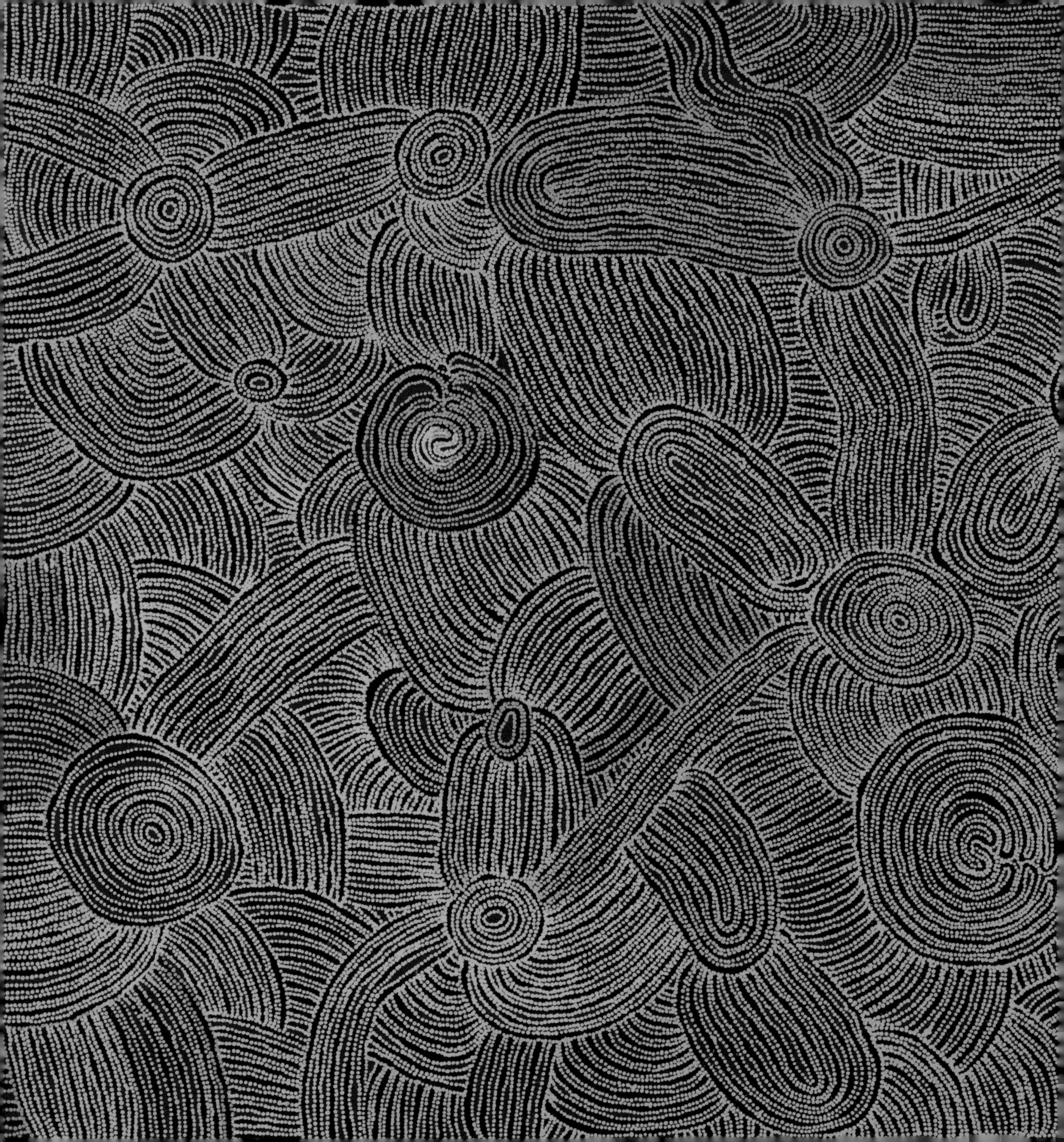

## Introduction

Craig Edwards' gift to ANU could not have come at a more timely moment. It coincides with a major reconfiguration of the campus that is well under way, and with the planned opening in early 2019 of the new centre, Kambri. The scale and extent of the building works at ANU has raised the question: "What is going to go into these new spaces that will open eyes and minds?"

As the result of Craig Edwards' extraordinary generosity, we now know that it will be visual art works that will be put front and centre. The message they communicate will be: you are on Aboriginal land. Permeating the entire campus, the works of art he has given to the University will make a representation, a tapestry, a huge narrative of Country. Country is not just about the here and now – about the land of the Ngunnawal and Ngambri people. It's also the lands that our students come from, where ANU academics have gone and walked with the local people, and the ancestral territory of the artists in the Edwards collection, who demonstrate through their paintings the importance of the knowledge they are willing to share.

Craig Edwards began collecting in the mid-1990s, at a time when the first wave of Western Desert painting had already achieved major international recognition. The painters of the first wave, whose story is told in Ian Mclean's inspirational essay, were almost all men, whereas the second wave, post-1995, saw the emergence of a cohort of senior women, most of whom had begun painting late in life, when they were already in their late 50s or 60s. Generally speaking, most of the paintings produced by those women depict their ancestral country, the stories handed down by their mothers, the traditional sites of food gathering and places where ceremonies are performed.

Prominent in the Edwards collection is a family of high achievers: Nyurapayia Nampitjinpa (Mrs Bennett) born 1935 and her half-sisters Tjawina Porter Nampitjinpa, born around 1940, and Esther Giles Nampitjinpa, born 1948. The Edwards collection features 28 works by the three sisters.

Tjawina Porter Nampitjinpa, *Untitled* 2012 (detail), acrylic on canvas, 183 x 244 cm

Naata Nungurrayi, born in 1932, became the matriarch of another great family of Western Desert artists: she was sister to Nancy Ross Nungurrayi and to George Tjungurrayi (both also present in the Edwards collection). By all standards, Naata is one of the most highly regarded Western Desert painters of our time. Her works are given pride of place in State and National collections and in many important exhibitions. She is highly sought-after by private collectors: she was nominated among the top 50 of Australia's most collectable artists by the *Australian Art Collector* magazine in 2004. The Edwards collection – and now ANU – is stupendously rich in her work: 34 paintings in all.

"It stirs in the heart of a nation" – that is how Ian Mclean describes the triumph of Western Desert art in his essay. We all know – we all should know – the impact that a work of art can have on us: there's a richness of communication. Ultimately it's not just about looking. We seek to understand the back-stories and as a result will deepen our connection with people across the country.

When the artists or their relatives, or people from their communities come to visit ANU and see the respect that is given to these art works, and when they recognise how these works have been made with such reverence and integrity of purpose, and how they have created such a powerful moment within our University space, I think those visitors will feel strengthened by the inspiration to continue and will understand the importance of sharing. This is not just a big donation – it is all about connection and sharing, and it has come from the heart. It is an enrichment to our community and it will impact on students and visitors to the campus for generations ahead.

Anne Martin

Director
Tjabal Indigenous Higher Education Centre
Australian National University

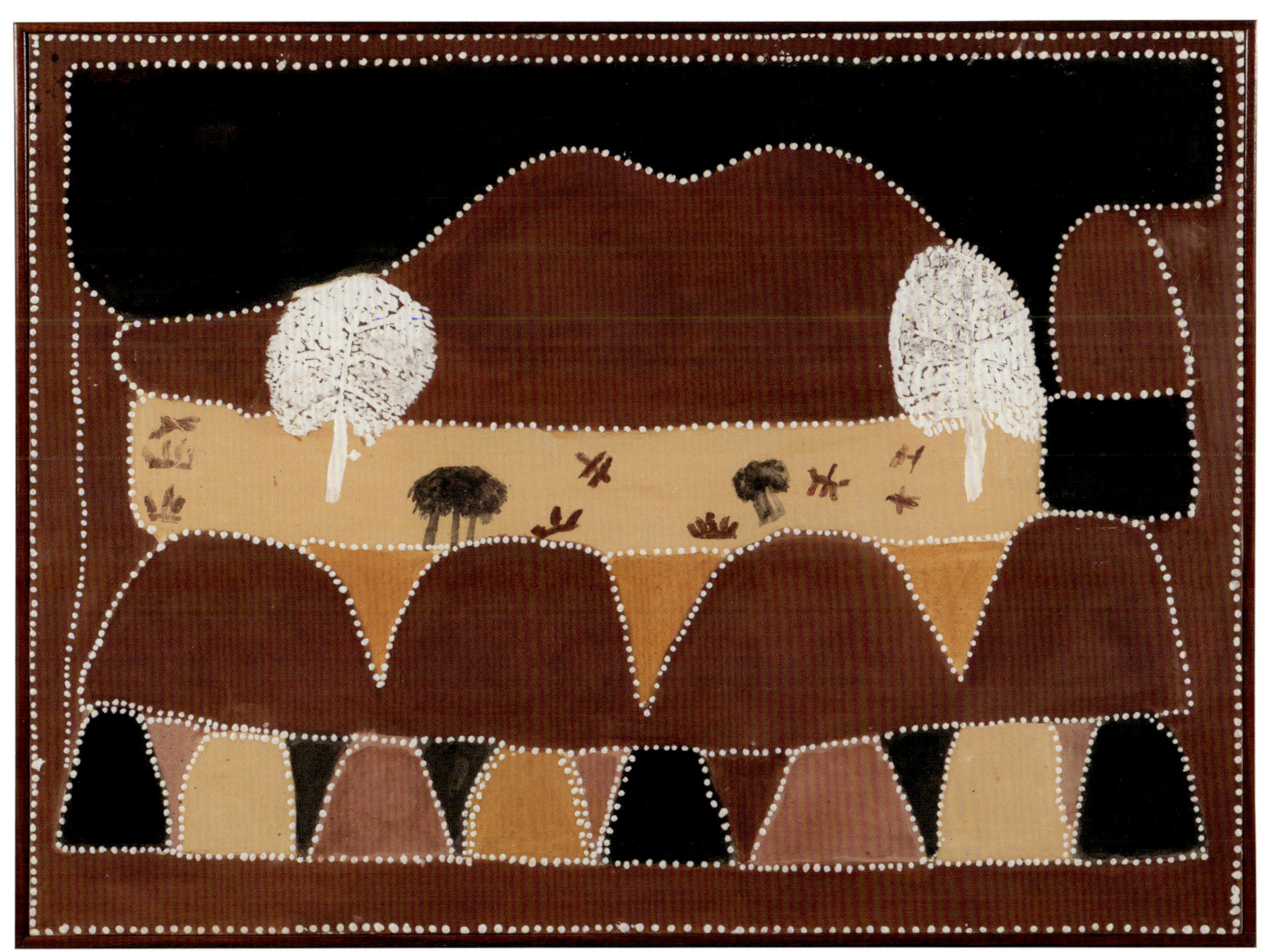

Queenie McKenzie, *Untitled (Artist's Country)* 1993, ochre on linen, 120 x 90 cm

Dorothy Napangardi, *Salt on Mina Mina* 2012,
acrylic on Belgian linen, 182 x 244cm

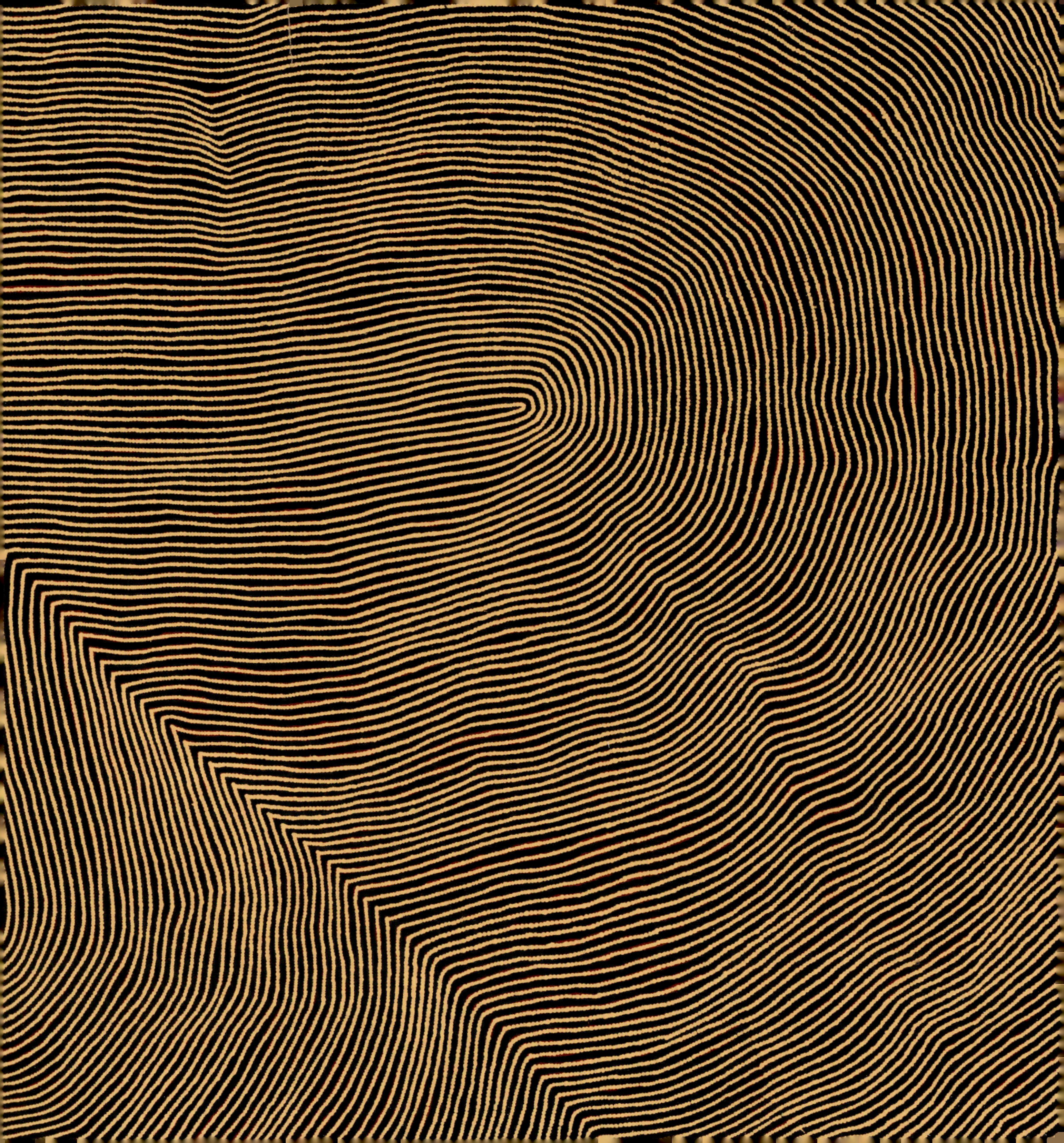

## Western Desert art and the Sublime

In mid-1971 an unassuming school project at the barely-known, newly-established Aboriginal settlement of Papunya (population about 1000) morphed into a catalyst that kick-started an art movement. This prosaic beginning concealed more than it revealed. There was no manifesto, plan or even intention, yet suddenly, like a rabbit out of the hat, the Western Desert art movement was born. Its first paintings are now its classic expressions – as if the movement emerged fully formed. A mystery for sure, but how does one unconceal origins that are nothing but sublime (i.e. beyond explanation, unrepresentable)? Dream-like, this mercurial art movement came as if from nowhere.

Perhaps those attuned to the supernatural saw it coming, for Papunya is a surreal place where the mysteries have a palpable presence. Its de Chirico-like landscape is a suitable playground of the gods; folded into deep time and Pythagorean configurations, it is an important site of the Honey-Ant Dreaming and the locus of a singular geometric symmetry. Situated close to the continental 'pole of inaccessibility' (the geographical point furthest from any coastline), Papunya is literally the midpoint, the pivot of this dry continent. Those sensitive to these hidden alignments would be alert to anything unusual. To them the extraordinarily heavy rain of 1971 must have seemed especially auspicious.

There was also something unreal and disconcerting about the quotidian realities of this shanty town. During the previous decade it had risen in the red dust to hold the last remnants of the Pintupi coming in from the west. Seething with discontent, the authorities and their Indigenous helpers struggled to assimilate them to the values of modernity and the Australian nation state. Papunya was at breaking point; riots had erupted – yet, invisible to the unknowing eye, beneath its chaotic appearance, there was an order based on tribal affiliations and authority. Like the honey ants growing fat from the bounty of rain, the Indigenous shamans who ordered this order were restless.

Warlimpirrnga Tjapaltjarri, *Untitled* 2008 (detail), acrylic on canvas, 183 x 244 cm

Being so new, Papunya was on few maps and unknown to the outside world. Even fewer heard the faint pop of the first Western Desert art set loose by the acrylic rainbows flickering on scraps of composition board and fibro. But a fire was lit, and as it began to blaze in the eyes of the artists, the more established Indigenous desert communities feared the worst. They did their best to put a lid on it, but even they would be converted. By the mid-1980s the art movement was a meteor shooting through the desert and onwards into the art world. In the 1990s it played a seminal role in transforming the paradigms of a Eurocentric art world hardened in its tastes, and by the end of the century it had truly arrived: a major retrospective exhibition opened at the Art Gallery of New South Wales called 'Papunya Tula Genesis and Genius', and professionally managed art centres had been established in most of the small hub communities across the desert regions of central and western Australia. With turnover in the millions of dollars and speculators circling from around the world, it had become an industry in the full sense of the term. Neither Australia nor any other country had ever seen anything like it.

Being so distant from the centres of power and art world discourse, Papunya's sudden fame defies the prescribed narratives of art history. This only adds to its mystery, setting its accounts apart from normal art historiography. Even the most prosaic of historians invariably express their wonder at its miraculousness. Nicolas Rothwell, alive to its significance, pronounced it 'Australia's only artistic revolution'.[1]

Not just an artistic revolution, the Western Desert art movement unsettled every dimension of modernism's historical continuum, not to mention the ideological assumptions of Australian art. With no herald, not even the most teleologically inclined minds could make much sense of it. Into the 1960s and '70s the imminent death of Australian Indigenous art had been the expert's prognosis, as if History had preordained its passing. This sudden bursting forth of Western Desert art in the contemporary art world is exemplary of what Foucault called a 'rift', a 'discontinuity' that with the force of divine intervention cuts through the existing order of things to reveal 'order in its primary state': 'the pure experience of order'.[2]

'The pure experience of order' – which is a principle without content – is a sublime phenomenon that is not easily apprehended, let alone described and analysed. Foucault suggested it was a subliminal *a priori* mental power that submits differences to an order, an ancestral systematising mechanism, an orderology. Its function is to create epistemologies or theories of knowledge, so that when a reigning epistemology collapses, an entirely new one will be released, as occurred with the Western Desert art movement.

•

Art is no stranger to miracles: indeed, it is its core business. There is an arsenal of terms and ideas to describe its affects, most of which allude to the concept of the sublime. The sublime is a catch-all term for the inexplicable and transcendental, which makes it a dangerous term for the historian, who practices the most-sober profession of scientific explication. But no amount of caution can avoid the sublimity that saturates the paintings made in the Great Painting Room at Papunya and also the movement's coming into being and triumph amidst the despair of Papunya. It moved Geoff Bardon to his very soul. Its first chronicler, the one closest to it and who named it, Bardon pronounced: 'This was the gift that time gave, and I know this, in my heart, for I was there'.[3]

Bardon experienced the twelve months between mid-1971 and mid-1972 as one of escalating spiritual revelation. Admittedly, he was very open to it. A devout Christian in search of esoteric knowledge, he knew that God spoke in a sublime, not reasoned cadence. He immediately recognised the sublimity of the scene. No doubting Thomas, for the rest if his life he felt a calling to be its witness.[4] His account of the movement, embellished in metaphors of the sublime, set the tone for much of its later critical reception. Possessed of a cinematic imagination, Bardon described Papunya in surreal but highly animated, visual and visceral terms. It was 'a hidden city … filled with twilight people', in which 'it was not only the blind who could not see' – and arriving on a late February night, in the 'deep, hot night' as 'millions of insects buzzed about the humble street lights that lit the desert village', he woke the next day to the sound of rain: 'There was a shimmering of wild, darkening purple-and-green forms … and a dancing, glistening feeling came from the stone walls of the mountains'.[5] The art, he said, was 'a kind of incandescence', 'a marvellous dream of the time', 'the glory'.[6] It all built to such intensity that in July 1972 he had a mental collapse: 'Even to speak of it now would be like living the time all over again; so the story will not be told, for it cannot'.[7]

While not all Western Desert paintings are equally sublime or even approach sublimity, sublimeness is its calling card, its brand, its myth. To this day sublimity is the aspiration of its artists, who hope that the ancestors will move their brushes as they once did in The Great Painting Room. The brand is as powerful as it's fitting, as it has a suitable mythical resonance: there is the First Peoples returning from the Golden Age to reclaim their birthright, the desert setting where the sublime attains its most metaphysical intensity, and the cosmological grandeur of the art's ancestral subjects and their renderings. It is a brand for the occasion and is used more than any other to sell the art. But is it a credible basis upon which to build an art history of the movement?

•

While the sublime is a classic art concept, it has been invoked so often that it has long been a cliché. By the 1970s an emerging postmodern generation dismissed it as a tired concept associated with outmoded notions of genius and freedom. Yet influential thinkers from Foucault and Lyotard to Derrida continued to draw on its conceptual conundrums and many artists could not let it go. This ambivalence, a sign that it harbours the inescapable contradictions of the contemporary condition, make it all the more interesting – and never more so given Western Desert art's assault on the ontological assumptions of the idea of Western art.

On the other hand, there is little doubt that invoking the sublime is a readymade means of pulling Western Desert art into the Western paradigm of modernism and a Western mindset – a mindset that characterises the age of colonialism and modernity. Should we not 'decolonise' the Western Desert sublime by explaining it within the Indigenous cosmologies of its making? Yet this very thought further entrenches the binary that the question intends to deconstruct. Further, to claim the sublime as a European idea misses its universal character and acquiesces to the Eurocentric imperative that wants everything for itself. Besides, Bardon did explain the art within Indigenous cosmologies, patiently transcribing the artists' descriptions of the ancestral narratives of each painting, which he and they believed were essential to the art's meaning and force. These stories, like Old Testament and ancient Greek myths, resonate with the sublime at its most romantic and archetypal. They are transgressive, tragic and terrifying, which is why they retain such appeal in modern times. Nor were the artists adverse to invoking feelings

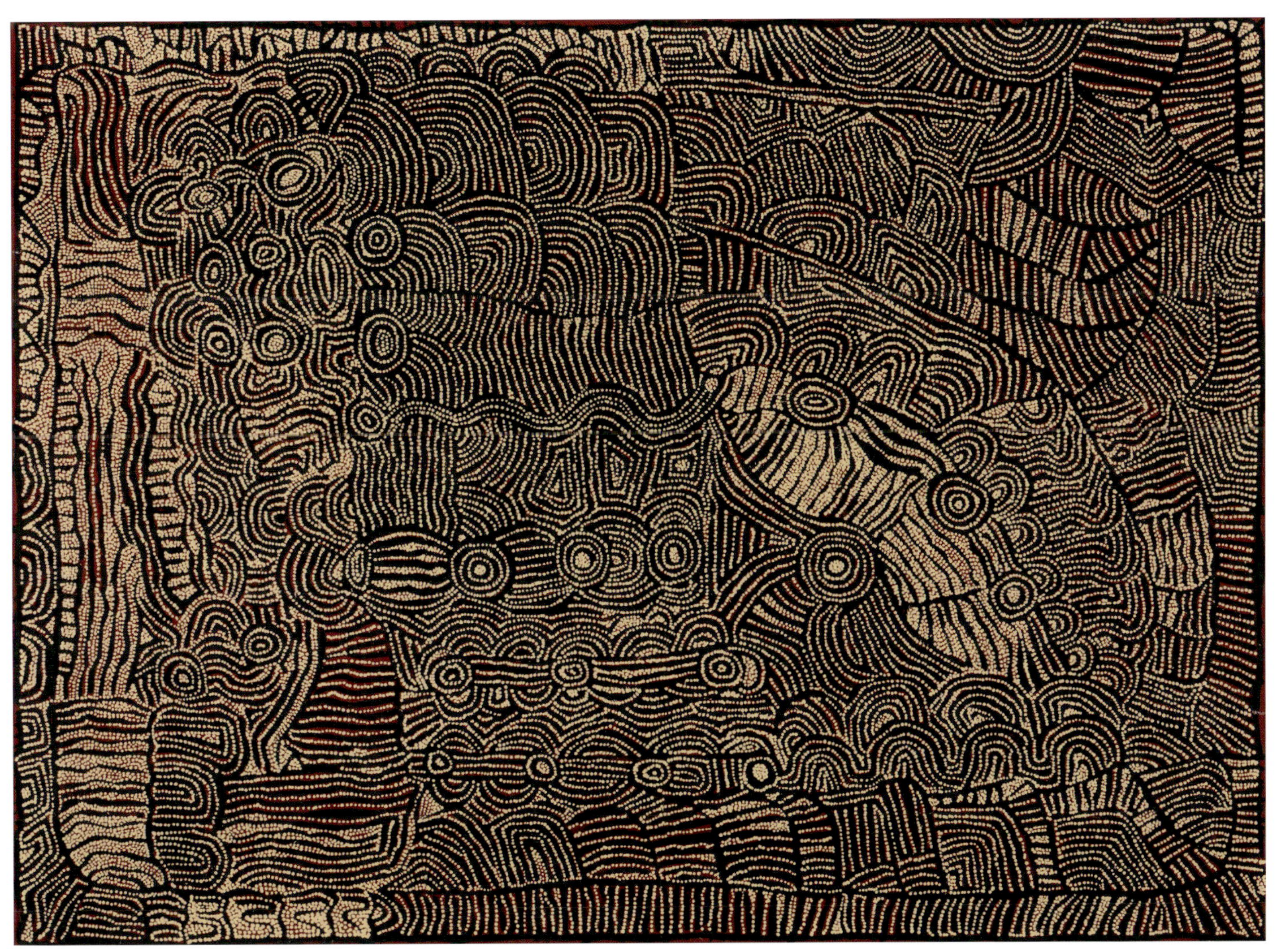

Nangawarra Ward Napurrula, *Untitled* 2009, acrylic on Belgian linen, 183 x 244 cm

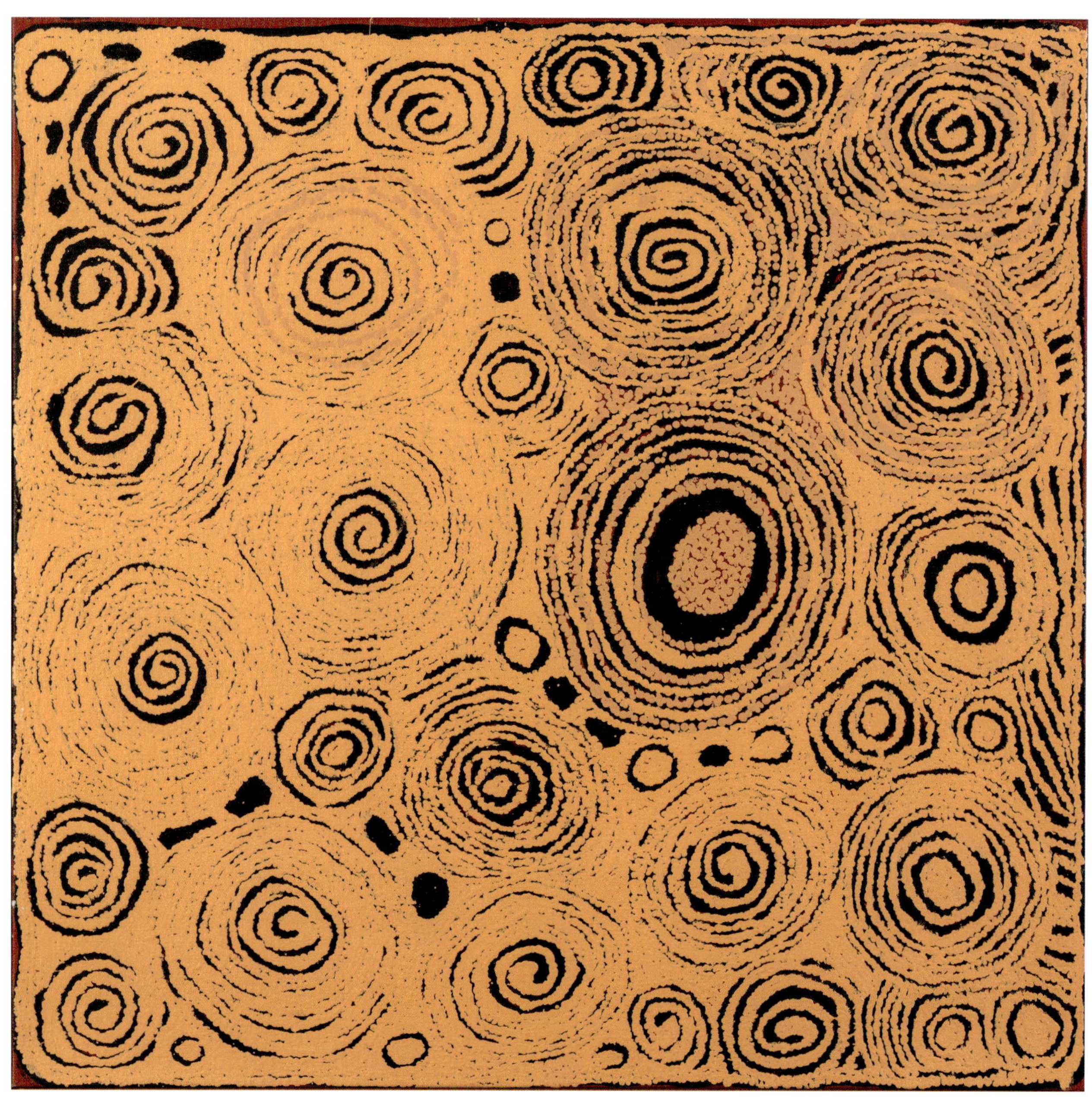

Nyurapayia Nampitjinpa (Mrs Bennett), *Kapi Tjukurrpa* 2006, acrylic on Belgian linen, 84 x 84 cm

associated with the sublime, especially the pioneers of the movement, many of whom were well-practised shamans.

Does this mean there is congruence between Indigenous evocations of the ancestral and the Western sublime that might thereby provide a pathway to a transcultural art history? What is the Western sublime, and does it open onto the esoteric terrain of Western Desert art?

## The Western sublime

During the eighteenth century the term 'sublime' took root in the Western imagination as a means to think beyond the limits of reason through an epistemology of feelings or embodied thoughts (i.e. sensibility as a faculty of knowledge), for which philosophers created a new field called aesthetics. Whatever its Western origins and contexts, the idea of the sublime was addressed in universal humanist terms. Over the next two centuries it would shape the theories and practices of modernism in Europe and elsewhere.

Like many modern European ideas and words, 'sublime' can be traced to a classical (ancestral) Greek or Latin text, which in this case is Longinus's *On the Sublime*. Likely written in the first century AD, it had little traction in Western philosophy until the latter sixteenth century when the Enlightenment's commitment to reason made it susceptible to Longinus's claim that the sublime is reason's antithesis. The sublime, said Longinus, 'does not convince the reason of the reader, but takes him out of himself'. Impervious to reason's logic, 'the Sublime, acting with an imperious and irresistible force, sways every reader whether he will or no'.[8] It acts not by argument but 'illuminates an entire subject with the vividness of a lightning-flash, and exhibits the whole power of the orator in a moment of time'.[9]

Longinus's treatise also struck a chord because it discussed the sublime as an attribute of literary style, thus making it amenable to the modern idea of aesthetics. Further, an ethical undercurrent drove its deliberations in which style rather than content or subject matter is a measure of the text's profundity and truth. Longinus claimed that a sublime style is only found in the greatest writers. Arousing the most profound and lofty emotions, it abhors ‘bombast’ at one extreme and ‘over-elaboration’ at the other. ‘We cannot’, he wrote, ‘pardon a tasteless grandiloquence’.[10] In order to distinguish between ‘the true and false Sublime’, Longinus asked: is this ‘gorgeous exterior a mere false and clumsy pageant, which if laid open will be found to conceal nothing but emptiness?’[11] The test of true sublimity, he said, is if the text extends the reader’s thoughts ‘beyond what is actually expressed’.[12]

The sublime was first popularised in Western discourse by several eighteenth-century English writers (from the 3rd Earl of Shaftesbury and Joseph Addison to Edmund Burke) who described it in terms of feelings aroused by nature rather than Longinus’s subject of literature. The nature they had in mind was the Swiss Alps, a wilderness (ancestral landscape) of soaring mountains and plunging valleys passed through on the Grand Tour of Italy’s art and classical ruins. The Alps, which were literally the sub (*sub*: at the foot of) lime (*limen*: threshold) of the Tour’s destination, established a conceptual opposition between the settled beauty of Italy’s avowedly humanist art set in picturesque countryside and the ‘agreeable horror’ of the Alps that took one’s breath away.[13] The opposition provided a means to rethink existing theories of subjectivity and the cosmos. A new cosmology, which would be identified with romanticism, was in the making. The German philosopher Immanuel Kant was the most profound and influential theorist of this modern sublime.

Kant shifted attention from sensations (of place or literary style) to the mind’s cognitive actions that translate sensations into the mental perceptions that underpin our representations of the world. According to him, the role of the sublime comes into play following failures in the normative conceptual and intuitive operations of such cognitive activity, opening us to seemingly deeper existential feelings of freedom and identity.

The weak link in cognitive operations, argued Kant, is its intuitive not conceptual procedures. While the latter are secured by general *a priori* categories in the faculty of understanding, and thereby produce determinate perceptions of space and time, the faculty of imagination that intuitively produces perceptions of space and time is not fool-proof. This is because its judgements are subject to the aesthetic faculty’s *a priori* sense of the beautiful, which are based on subjective feelings of pleasure. We deem spatial and temporal perceptions pleasurable (and so beautiful) when they create the impression of the 'union of taste with reason',[14] as if they are 'preadapted to our power of judgement' (i.e. without need of determinate *a priori* concepts). In this way a single aesthetic intuition can represent our understanding of the world as reasonable 'without our indulging in any refinements of thought'.[15] However, this happy correspondence between taste and reason collapses when vast magnitudes cannot be represented in a single aesthetic intuition. Such 'an outrage on the imagination',[16] as Kant put it, invokes the sublime, which transforms the pain and incomprehension of this 'outrage' into a new sort of pleasure.

The sublime, says Kant, is evidence of 'a faculty of mind transcending every standard of sense' – which he called the pure 'supersensible' feeling of the (mathematical) sublime.[17] This, if we follow Kant, is what was experienced on the Grand Tour. Amongst the classical ruins of the Italian campagna, the imagination enjoyed the happy equilibrium of the beautiful, but the sublime emotions experienced traversing the Alps brought a profounder pleasure – profounder because it revealed that the cognitive operations of reason are more deeply embedded in the mind, more ancestral, than the outer consciousness of sensations. Here is a purer, more autonomous transcendental feeling beyond the rule of taste, and as such it touches the very identity of Being – akin to what Foucault called 'order in its primary state' and 'the pure experience of order'.[18] Hence, as Kant concluded, 'aesthetic judgement refers not merely, as a judgement of taste, to the beautiful, but also, as springing from a higher intellectual feeling, to the sublime'.[19] He attributed this 'higher' sense of the sublime to 'the might of the mind', which he argued is 'far stronger and more enduring ... than the stimulus afforded by sensible representations' of the outside world.[20] It is an experience many feel as intensely spiritual and harbouring an inner freedom.

Because Kant considered the sublime an affirmation of the self and its freedom in the face of incomprehension and danger, his theory of the mind was an idea for its times. Published in three volumes as the French Revolution unfolded to his excitement, his invocation of the sublime was a means to start again. In the wake of the French Revolution it would greatly influence thinking about art, identity and being, as well as theories of knowledge.

## The Western Desert sublime

Considered in Kantian terms, the Western Desert sublime is an affirmation of Indigenous being and freedom in the face of a danger. This was a new type of danger: not one of surviving in the desert or the ruthlessness of the colonial agenda, but its aftermath and the seductions of modernity. At this moment in the post-WWII period, the desert tribes had reached an impasse. Those living traditional lives had been greatly reduced over the previous fifty years as large numbers had been attracted to the modernity of the missions on the periphery of the desert and, since the 1950s, to government communities such as Papunya.

Bardon described the Papunya he saw in 1971 in totally desolate terms – 'a place of emotional loss and waste, with an air of casual cruelty',[21] of endemic disease, violence and high mortality, its inhabitants completely dispirited:

> ... a mere thought shadow of peoples, many of whose ancestors had been massacred, poisoned or starved to death over a period of some generations after their contact with Europeans ... a place of abundant hatred and distress.[22]

However, the ritual leaders of these desert people had more pressing problems on their mind. Their (i.e. the ancestors') authority was threatened. In the settlement they watched helplessly as their children were educated in a Western curriculum that had no room for their epistemologies. Bardon provided them with an opportunity to meet modernity's revolutions with their own aesthetic revolution. It was a means for the ritual leaders to re-assert agency and ownership of their present lives and being.

That the ritual leaders turned to the aesthetic attributes of the sublime in such desperate times is not unexpected in either Kantian theory – in which the sublime is the action of last resort – or their own traditions. Western Desert art traditions, like all art traditions, are well attuned to the sublime, especially in its more mystical, secretive expressions. The chief shaman, who is the chief artist, is always the last hope in moments of extreme danger. Western Desert rituals include secret symbolism and also a strong undercurrent of mesmerising patterns and rhythms that sweep initiates away. These disorientating patterns – a principal attribute of Western Desert painting to this day – are constructed as fields of ambiguity in order to interfere with the linearity of the imagination's spatial and temporal intuitions. This dream-like disruption of normative intuitions of space/time is associated in all traditional cultures with ancestral presence – terror-inducing but, if like the shaman you keep your nerve, sublime.

## The birth of the Western Desert art movement

There were two pivotal elements in the initial formation of the Western Desert art movement at Papunya: Geoff Bardon, who arrived at the beginning of the school year in February 1971 as a new teacher; and a group of ritual leaders in their sixties – Mick Tjakamarra, Walter Tjampatjimpa, Tom Onion Tjapangati, Bert Tjakamarra and Tutuma Tjapangati. The movement was born from a transcultural alliance between Bardon and these ritual leaders, whom Bardon began to meet from about May (1971) as his presence and enthusiasm as the art teacher was increasingly felt in the Indigenous community. The alliance was cemented by Kaapa Tjampitjinpa, Johnny Warangkula Tjupurrula and Mick Namerari Tjapaltjarri, each aged around fifty, who associated with the ritual leaders as well as the school groundsmen, Billy Stockman Tjapaltjarri and Long Jack Phillipus – each of whom was a generation younger than the ritual leaders.

Only later did Bardon understand the role of the ritual leaders. Kaapa was the main painter at Papunya, and he, Warangkula and Namerari met with the ritual leaders in an abandoned building that served as Kaapa's studio but in effect was an underground church in which the Old Men socialised, schemed and passed on their knowledge. Bardon's initial entrée into this group was as the hunting companion of Warangkula and Namerari. Young enough to be their son, Bardon, who had just turned thirty, was very much the junior partner.

Abandoning the education department curriculum, Bardon instead sought, with much frustration, to entice the children to draw traditional Western Desert patterns. Intrigued, the ritual leaders took to sunning themselves outside his classroom as if bemused by his aberrant aspirations or maybe keeping an eye on the children so they wouldn't step out of line. Perhaps the children felt their eyes, for Bardon was frustrated in his efforts. Unable to get them to paint Pintupi-style murals under the school, Bardon and his assistant, the Arrernte man Obed Raggett, painted the first meaningless

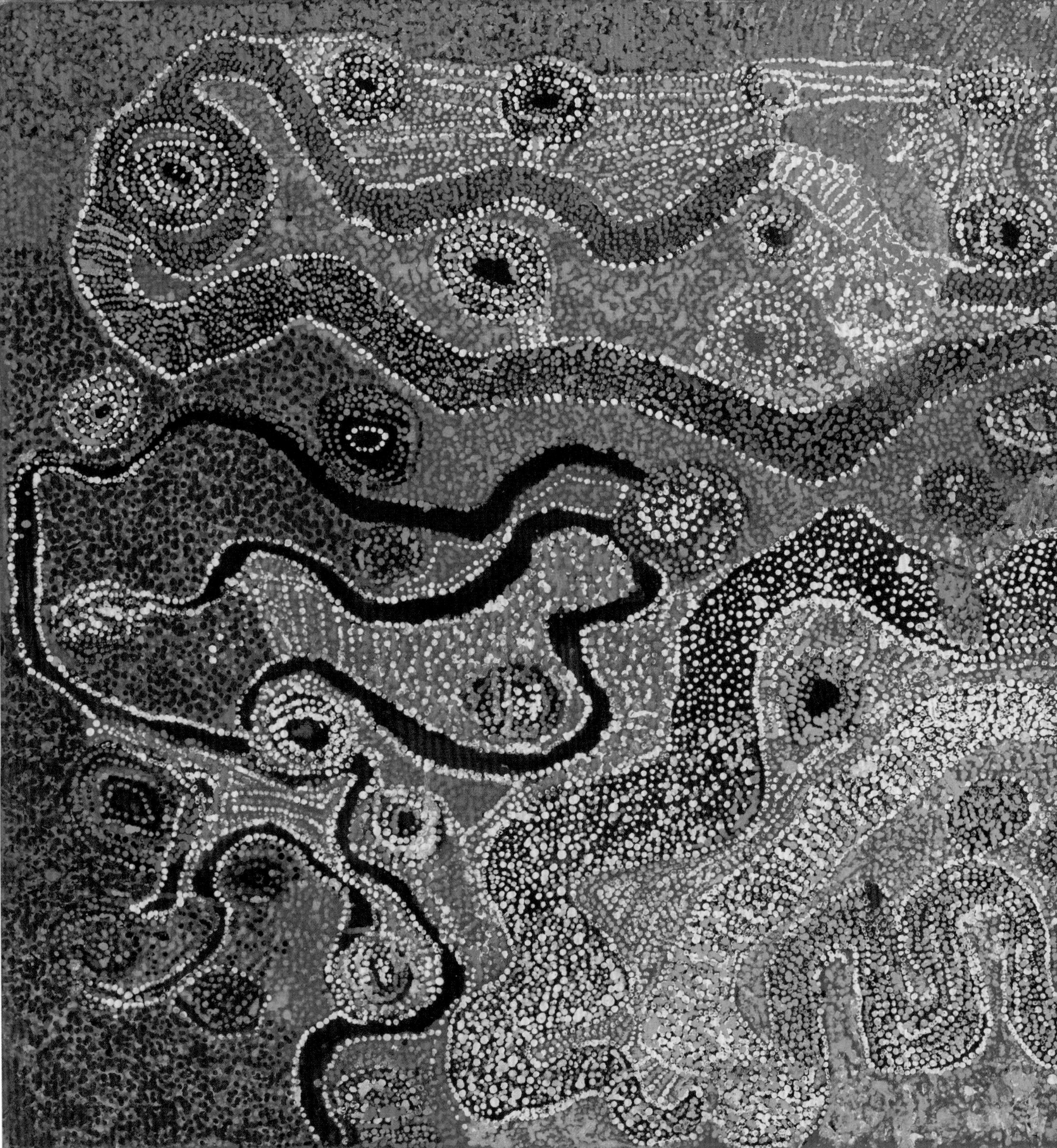

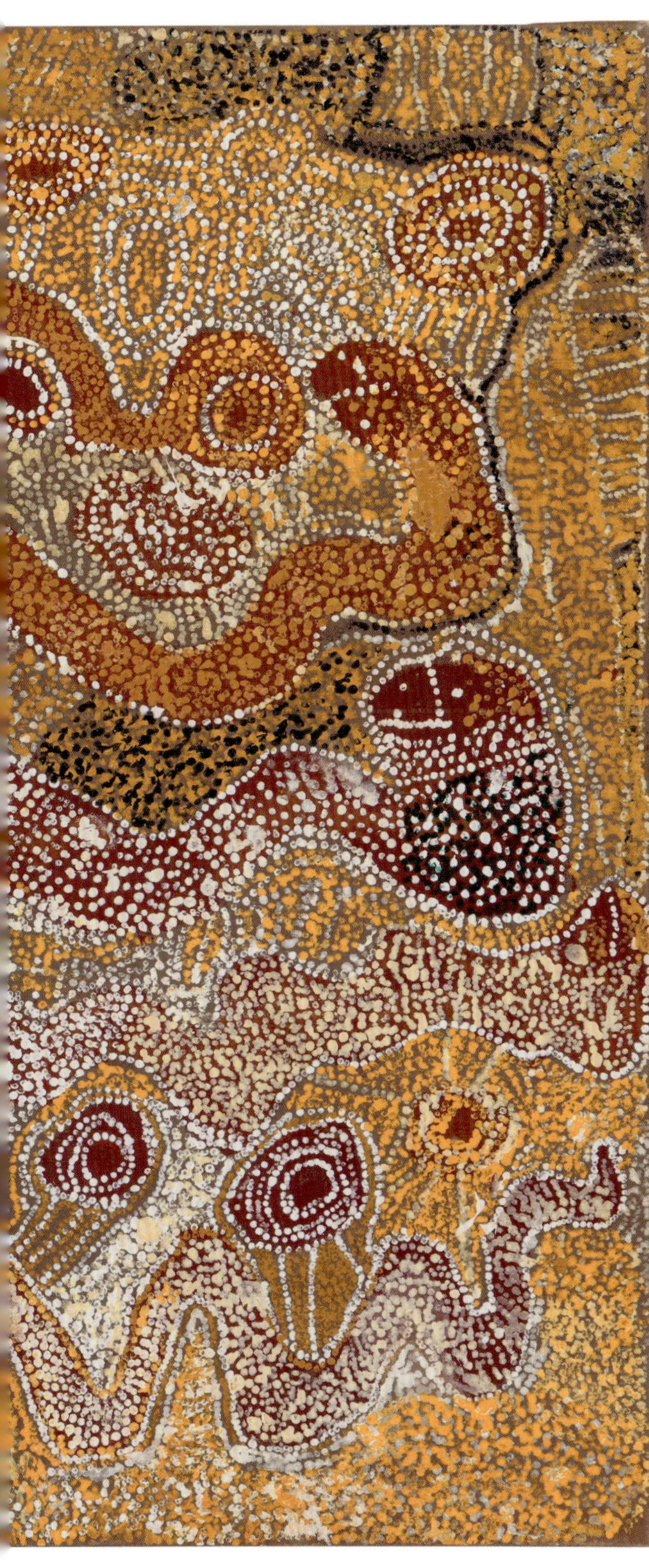

Wimmitji Tjapangati, *Yirriwalli* 1989,
acrylic on Belgian linen, 89 x 120 cm

(purely decorative) mural, after which Long Jack and Billy Stockman stepped in and helped with the second – a Widow Dreaming story. During this period, in July and August, half a dozen murals were painted, each conceived by the men to satisfy different tribal factions at Papunya. By then tremendous community interest had been aroused in the mural project, as Indigenous perspectives were seemingly made part of the school curriculum.

The ritual leaders conceived the final and largest mural, the local Honey Ant story, and had their man, Kaapa, organise its painting. It was, wrote Bardon, 'The climatic public affirmation of Aboriginal identity at Papunya':[23] 'This was', claimed Bardon, 'the beginning of the Western Desert painting movement when, led by Kaapa, the Aboriginal men saw themselves in their own image and before their very own eyes, and upon a European building'.[24] As the murals were being painted some of the men began to paint in the back of the classroom, where they made a space for themselves. Even the ritual leaders began to come. 'This is where the painting movement began', said Bardon: 'the steady, full steps of the painters coming up the stairs and then a great silence as they sat down to work'.[25]

Bardon described the impact of the mural on the men and the community in sublime terms: 'Truly something strange and marvellous had begun … there were enormous roars, and wild acclamation and dancing and singing, in the great camps at night, and a sense of our best affirmations coming to life'.[26] However, neither the Honey Ant nor other murals were sublime artworks. They did not, for example, match the intense feelings of the paintings in the restricted Men's Museum painted at Yuendumu at exactly the same time, and where initiation ceremonies were undertaken. The Papunya school murals were intended as pedagogical exercises to teach children the stories of their ancestors, not as sublime ritualistic expressions that initiated young men into their mysteries – nor were the paintings made in the second half of the year in the classroom intended to do so either.[27]

However, after Bardon got his murals in this year of record rains, the ritual leaders, the rain men, made it known to Bardon that they were expecting something in return: not the pedagogical art made for the children, but affirmations of their sublime power. 'There was', said Bardon, 'a felt need among some of the painters for "powerful" stories, or "initiation" stories involving blood, kidneys, sex and general spiritual invocations for water and bush tucker'.[28]

In the new year Bardon arranged for a men's-only studio – what he called the Great Painting Room. Here, he said, the men worked 'together as a kind of confraternity'; more men joined so that some twenty-five, mostly Pintupi, 'sat in a mysterious order of skin relationships', each 'facing the door ... no one sat with his back to the door'.[29] From here surged

> a veritable flood of brilliant paintings; the men in groups about the darkened, cave-like interior of the galvanised iron circle of a shed, singing and roaring out to their creations ... forms irradiating into new forms ... with many Pintupi being overcome, and everywhere in the room completed paintings of immense accomplishment.[30]

These works were in great contrast to the pedagogical paintings made at the school in 1971, where each man had painted silently as if in his own world. Then 'the men showed no concern for the technical quality of each other's work and seldom discussed what they individually painted.'[31] But in the Great Painting Room the atmosphere of elation and sense of a common cause was very different: 'As 1972 progressed there was even more intense criticism and appreciation by each artist of the others' stories', and the 'wild exchanges in Pintupi among the men was often a lambasting of one or other painter for what he had not been able to do'.[32] This 'rising of the painters' spirits in 1972', said Bardon, 'made the painters new men, like warriors of old, and in many ways they were quite fearless about the stories they painted in the Great Painting Room'.[33] The Western Desert sublime had arrived.

### Beyond the sublime

As with any art that has claims on the sublime, there is much more to Western Desert art than sublimity. Sublimity is an exalted thing but it is also limited in its reach. As an aesthetic category it reveals itself as pure feeling. Fragile and ephemeral, like a rainbow it easily disperses. Worse, its autonomy and passivity, which is a necessary feature of its aloof authority and transcendental power, paradoxically leaves it available as a spiritual resource to whoever falls under its spell and also makes it easy prey to ideology and myth. Ideology desublimates spiritual power into religious dogma, mythical narratives, moral laws and political power, which underpin the social contract that art movements, like political, religious and even sporting movements, need in order to maintain their integrity and belief. It would be wrong to see such desublimation as a perversion or depletion of the sublime's spiritual power (which is without limit); rather, it is an expression, measure and indeed demonstration of it. The Western Desert sublime shows its power today as the brand that local Indigenous nations use in their struggles for sovereignty against the Australian nation state – quite literally as evidence in land rights claims, but more broadly as an assertion of cultural identity in the face of modernity.

The shift from the sublime to myth was already evident in the Great Painting Room as the men felt their strength returning. They 'really loved', Bardon said, his exhortations that 'we must "beat the big whitefella artists everywhere all over the place long way everywhere"'.[34] Far from being lost in the pure feeling of the sublime, the men were intent on gaining agency by modernising their ritual traditions. The mark of modernism in all traditions is the secularisation of religious art traditions through the transformation of the symbolism that underpinned religious dogma by heightening its abstract sublime affects. This was the great achievement of what occurred in the Great Painting Room in 1972 – led, argued Bardon, by Warangkula – and it resulted in a movement of increasingly abstract art.

Ironically, if by 1990 Western Desert art became the brand of Indigenous art, a measure of its political success is that it had also became the brand of the Australian nation state – one of its most iconic contemporary products and markers of identity. The Western Desert sublime is now also the Australian sublime, as if Bardon's exhortations to "beat the big whitefella artists everywhere all over the place long way everywhere" were realised.

If Western Desert art has in a short time gone from sublimity to myth, it is also very much a fact, impressed upon us by the fecundity of the art movement in that great rain or pouring-forth of paintings produced by so few people, which only serves to reinforce its mythic presence. In this respect Western Desert art is the closest thing contemporary Australians have to Gallipoli. Like Gallipoli it is a founding event that promises, in this case, to remake the nation in a different hue. Western Desert painting now appears wherever the nation seeks to show itself, from Qantas planes to the office walls of politicians and mining company executives. Here it serves the larger redemptive role of repatriating the nation's original sin of conquest – a repatriation forged in postcolonial hope, not the wars of Empire. Here, as if its arrival projects an afterimage of the id, the sublime emotion of Western Desert art serves a new myth in the making. Turned away from the objective conditions of colonialism – which can be no more apparent than in remote Indigenous communities such as Papunya – it faces towards a new subject that stirs in the heart of the nation.

Professor Ian McLean
Hugh Ramsay Chair in Australian Art History
University of Melbourne

Bibliography

Addison, Joseph. *Remarks on Several Parts of Italy, &c. In the Years 1701, 1702, 1703.* London: J. and R. Tonson, 1718.

Bardon, Geoffrey. "The Gift That Time Gave: Papunya Early and Late, 1971-72 and 1980." In M*ythscapes: Aboriginal Art of the Desert from the National Gallery of Victoria*, edited by Judith Ryan, 10-17. Melbourne: National Gallery of Victoria, 1989.

Bardon, Geoffrey. *Papunya Tula: Art of the Western Desert*. Marlston: J. B. Books, 1991.

Bardon, Geoffrey and Bardon, James. *Papunya: A Place Made after the Story: The Beginnings of the Western Desert Painting Movement*. Carlton: The Miegunyah Press, 2004.

Carter, Paul. "The Enigma of a Homeland Place: Mobilising the Papunya Tula Painting Movement 1971-1972." In *Papunya Tula: Genesis and Genius*, edited by Hetti Perkins, and Hannah Fink, 247-57. Sydney: Art Gallery of New South Wales, 2000.

Foucault, Michel. *The Order of Things: An Archaeology of the Human Sciences*. New York: Vintage Books, 1994. Les Mots et les choses, 1966, first English publication 1970.

Kant, Immanuel. *The Critique of Judgement*. Translated by James Creed Meredith. Oxford: Clarendon Press, 1952.

Longinus. *On the Sublime*. Translated by H. L. Havell. London: Macmillan & Co., 1890.

McLean, Ian. "The Gift That Time Gave: Myth and History in the Western Desert Painting Movement." In *Cambridge Companion to Australian Art History*, edited by Jaynie Anderson, 180-92. Cambridge: Cambridge, 2011.

Rothwell, Nicolas. "Sea Change in the Desert." *The Australian*, November 12 2004, B12.

---

1 Nicolas Rothwell, "Sea Change in the Desert," *The Australian*, November 12 2004.
2 Michel Foucault, *The Order of Things: An Archaeology of the Human Sciences* (New York: Vintage Books, 1994), xxi.
3 Geoffrey Bardon, "The Gift That Time Gave: Papunya Early and Late, 1971-72 and 1980," in *Mythscapes: Aboriginal Art of the Desert from the National Gallery of Victoria*, ed. Judith Ryan (Melbourne: National Gallery of Victoria, 1989), 16.
4 See Ian McLean, "The Gift That Time Gave: Myth and History in the Western Desert Painting Movement," in *Cambridge Companion to Australian Art History*, ed. Jaynie Anderson (Cambridge: Cambridge, 2011).
5 Geoffrey Bardon, *Papunya Tula: Art of the Western Desert* (Marlston: J. B. Books 1991), 10.
6 "The Gift That Time Gave: Papunya Early and Late, 1971-72 and 1980."
7 *Papunya Tula: Art of the Western Desert*, 46.
8 Longinus, *On the Sublime*, trans. H. L. Havell (London: Macmillan & Co., 1890), 2.
9 Ibid., 3.
10 Ibid., 5.
11 Ibid., 11.
12 Ibid., 12.
13 This expression, first used by Joseph Addison, was widely repeated: Joseph Addison, *Remarks on Several Parts of Italy, &c. In the Years 1701, 1702, 1703* (London: J. and R. Tonson, 1718), 261.
14 Ibid., 74.
15 Immanuel Kant, *The Critique of Judgement*, trans. James Creed Meredith (Oxford: Clarendon Press, 1952), 91.
16 Ibid., 91.
17 Ibid., 98.
18 Foucault, *The Order of Things: An Archaeology of the Human Sciences*, xxi.
19 Ibid., 33.
20 Ibid., 124.
21 Bardon, *Papunya Tula: Art of the Western Desert*, 10.
22 Geoffrey Bardon and James Bardon, *Papunya: A Place Made after the Story: The Beginnings of the Western Desert Painting Movement* (Carlton: The Miegunyah Press, 2004), 6.
23 Ibid., 16.
24 Quoted in Paul Carter, "The Enigma of a Homeland Place: Mobilising the Papunya Tula Painting Movement 1971-1972," in *Papunya Tula: Genesis and Genius*, ed. Hetti Perkins, and Hannah Fink (Sydney: Art Gallery of New South Wales, 2000), 253.
25 Bardon, *Papunya Tula: Art of the Western Desert*, 15.
26 Quoted in Carter, "The Enigma of a Homeland Place: Mobilising the Papunya Tula Painting Movement 1971-1972," 253.
27 Ibid.
28 Bardon, *Papunya: A Place Made after the Story: The Beginnings of the Western Desert Painting Movement*, 23.
29 Ibid., 27.
30 Ibid., 29.
31 Bardon, *Papunya Tula: Art of the Western Desert*, 24.
32 Ibid., 32.
33 Bardon, *Papunya: A Place Made after the Story: The Beginnings of the Western Desert Painting Movement*, 29.
34 Ibid., 32.

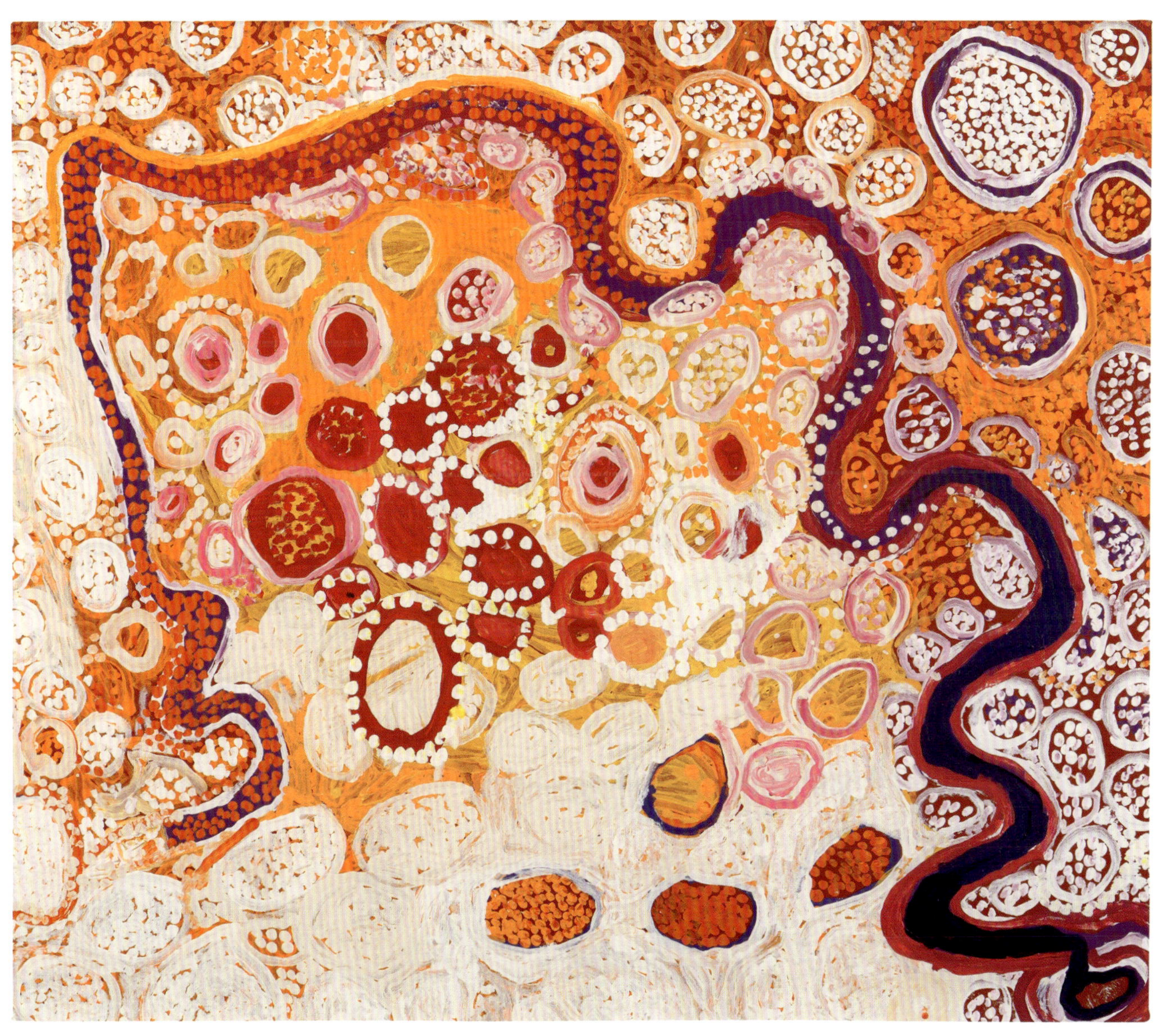

Tiger Palpatja, *Untitled* 2011, acrylic on Belgian linen, 91 x 102 cm

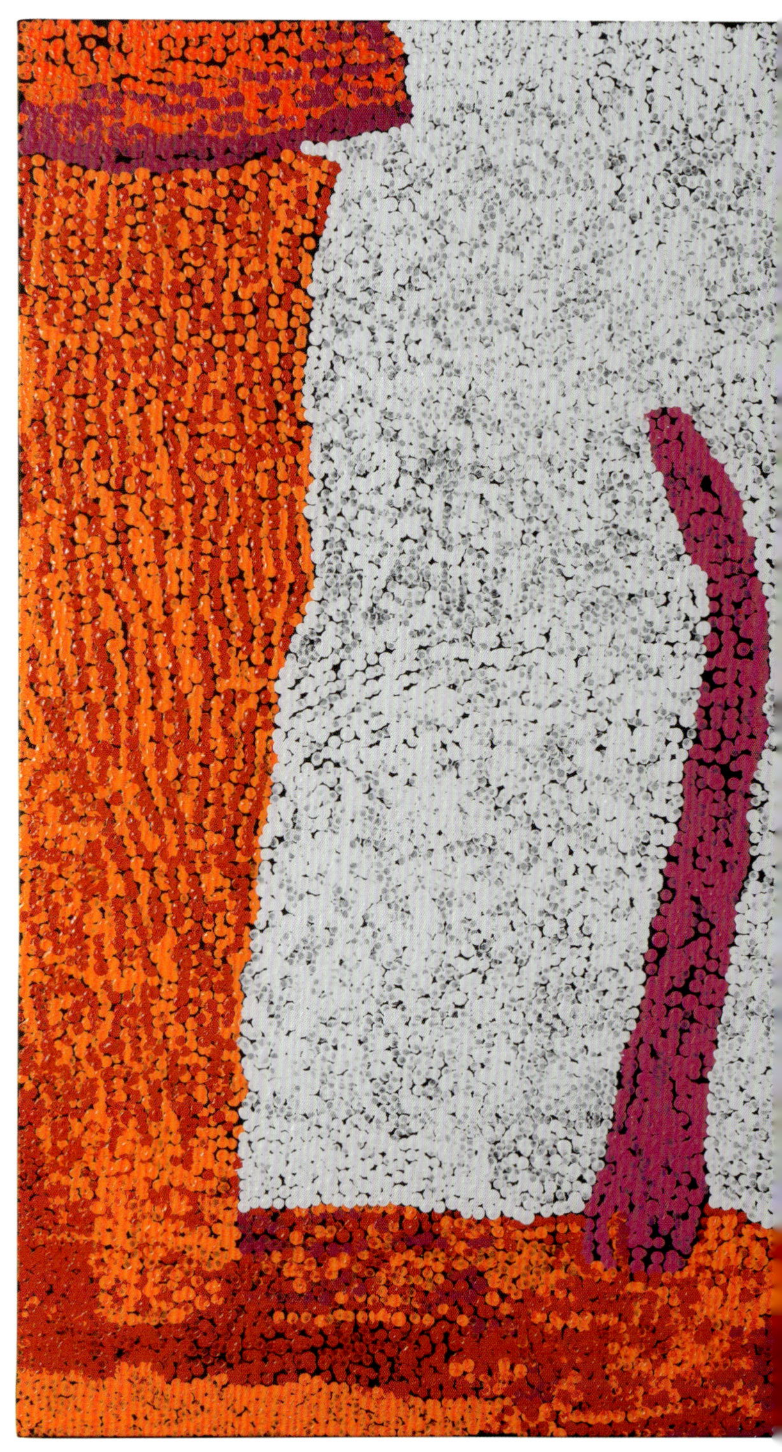

Yannima Pikarli Tommy Watson, *Untitled* 2014, acrylic on Belgian linen, 244 x 152 cm

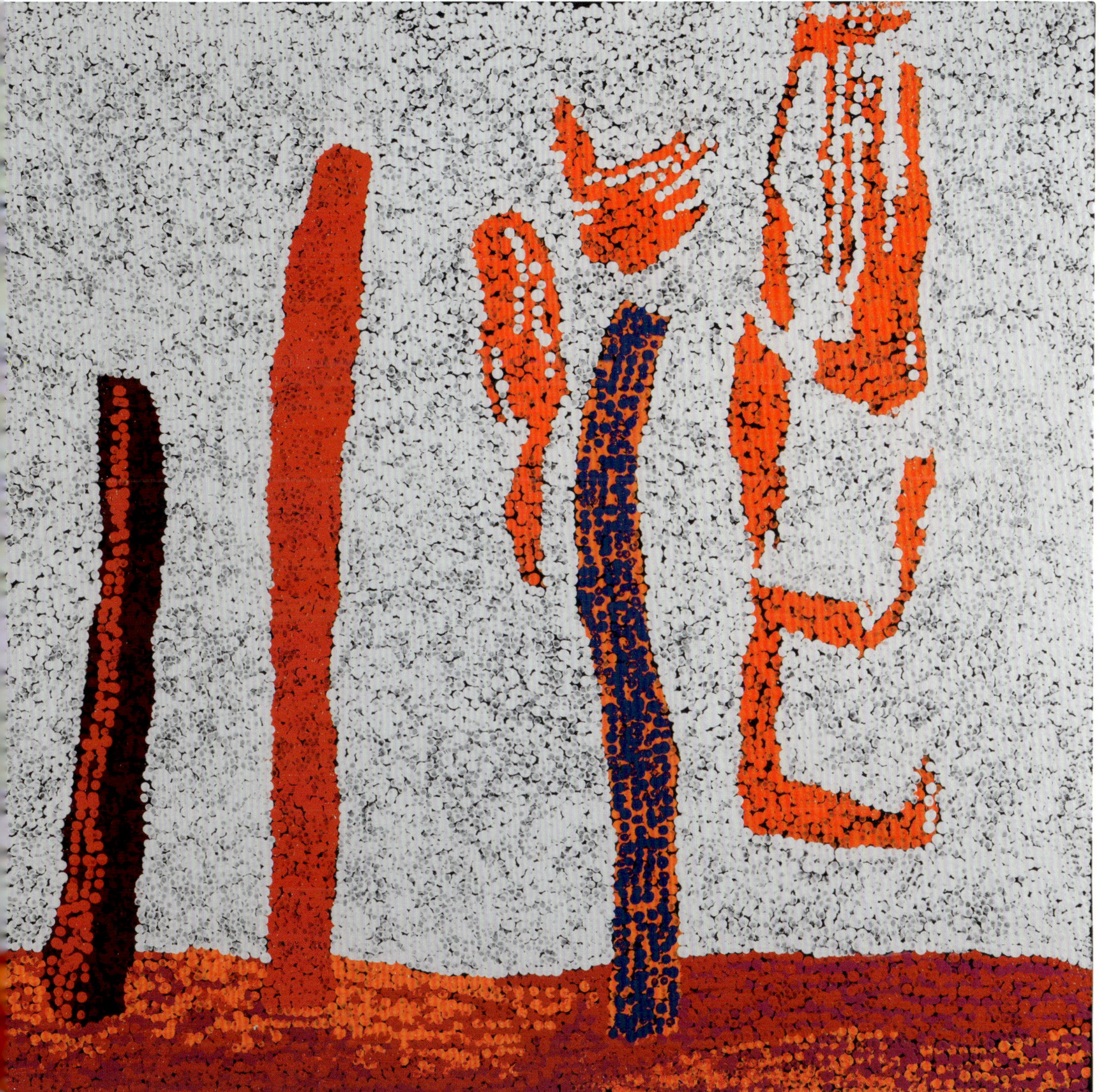

Naata Nungurrayi, *Marrapinti* 2014, acrylic on Belgian linen, 183 x 244 cm

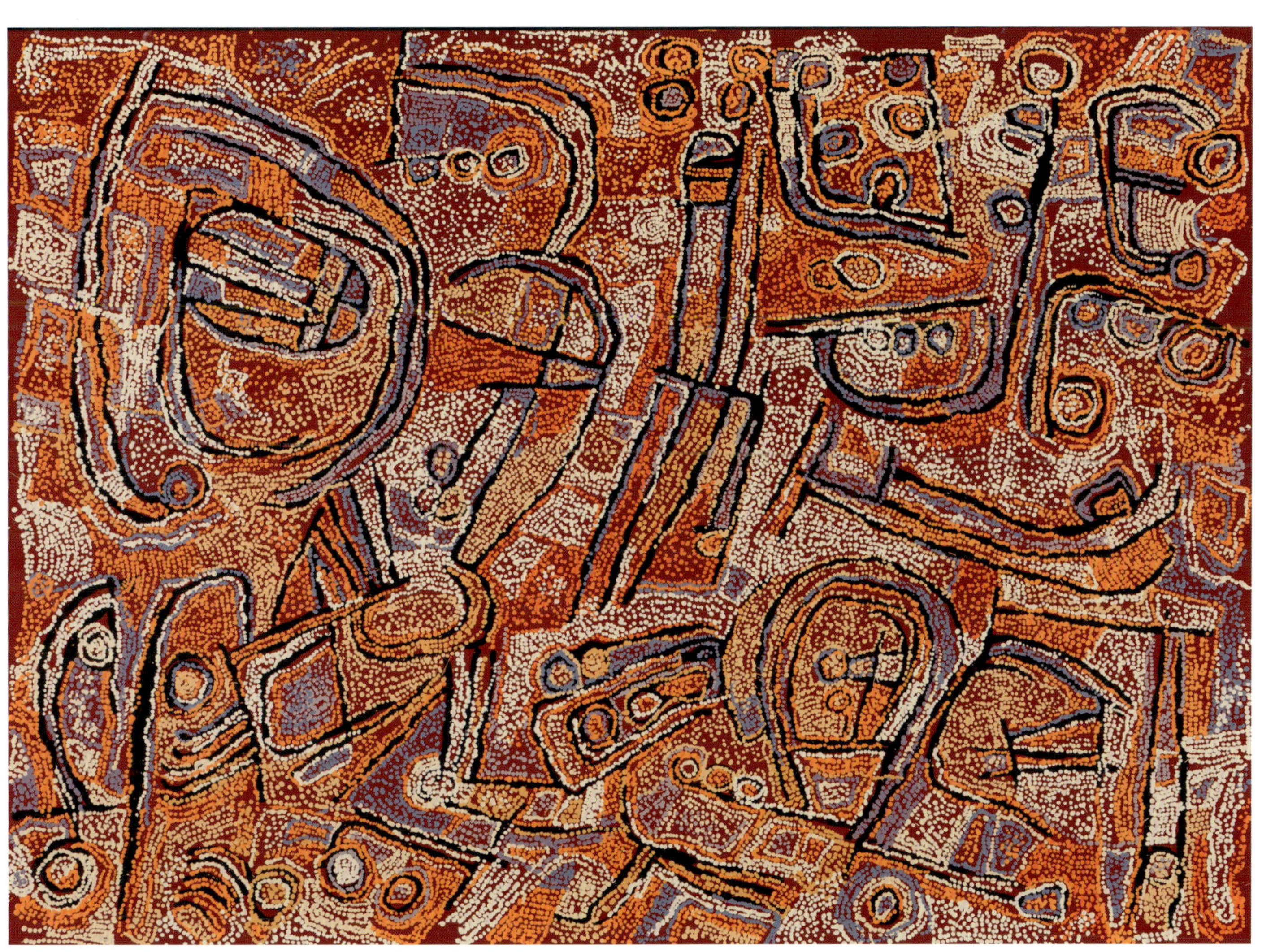

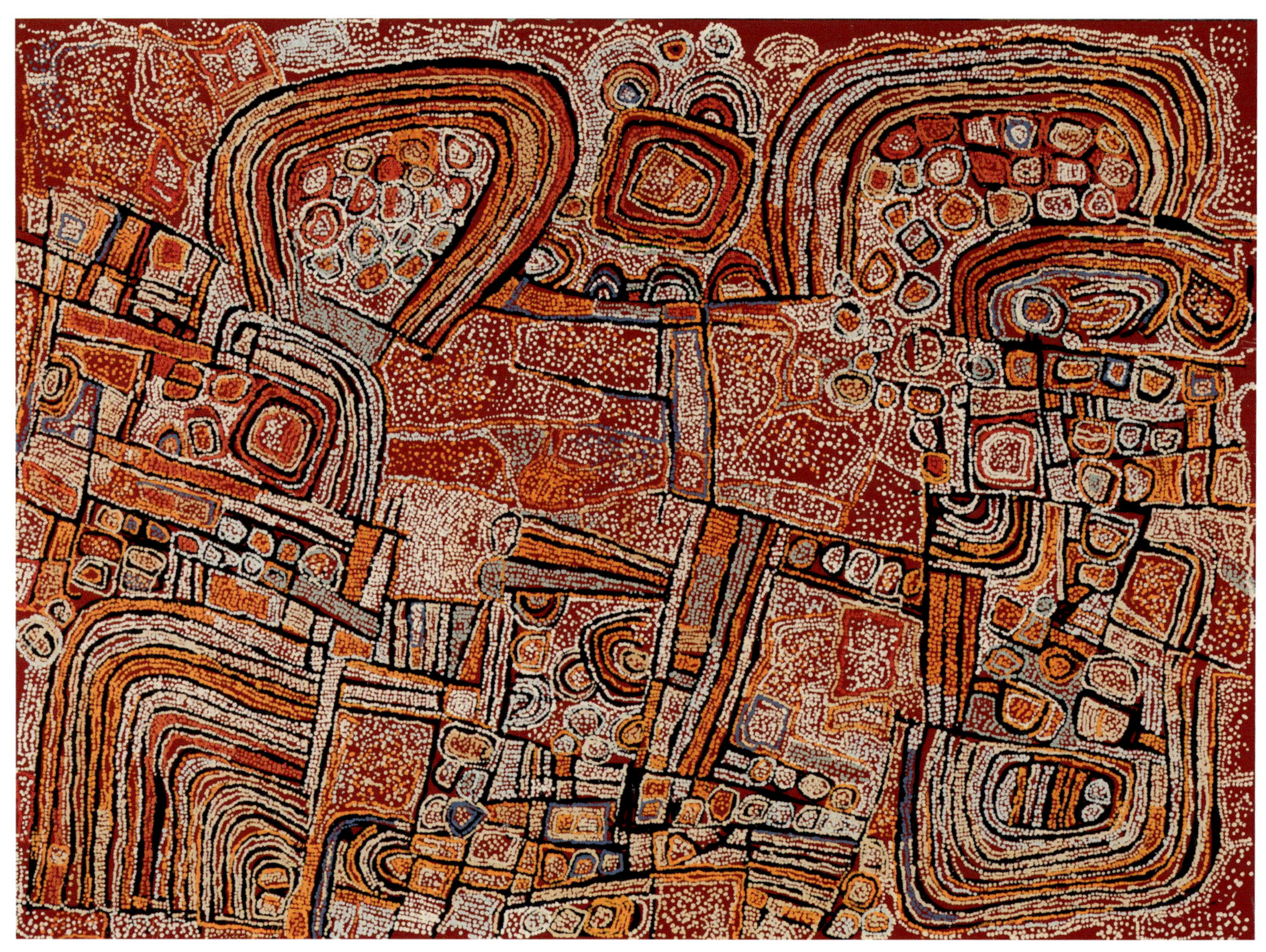

Naata Nungurrayi, *Marrapinti* 2012, acrylic on Belgian linen, 183 x 244 cm

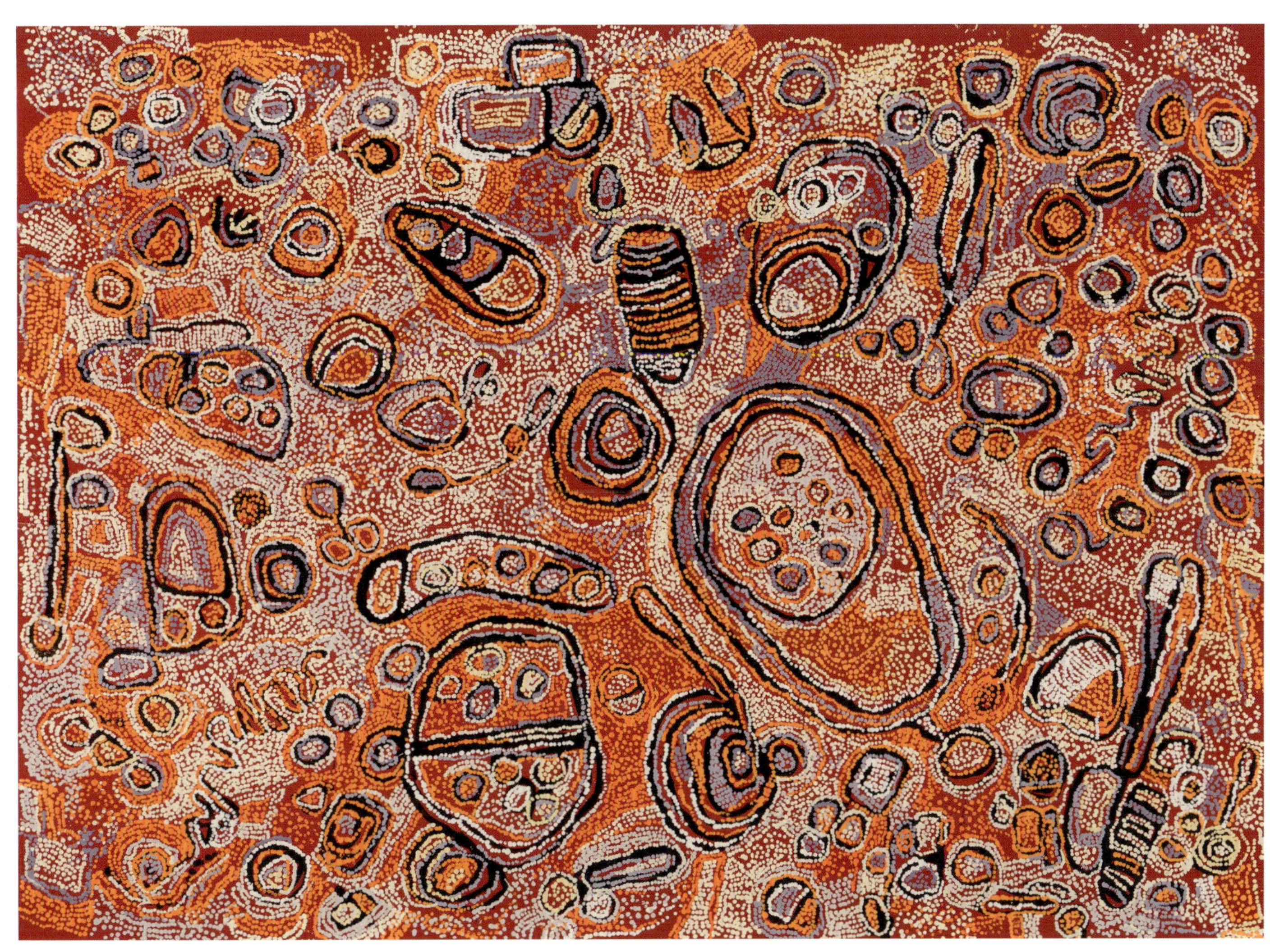

Naata Nungurrayi, *Marrapinti* 2015, acrylic on Belgian linen, 183 x 244 cm

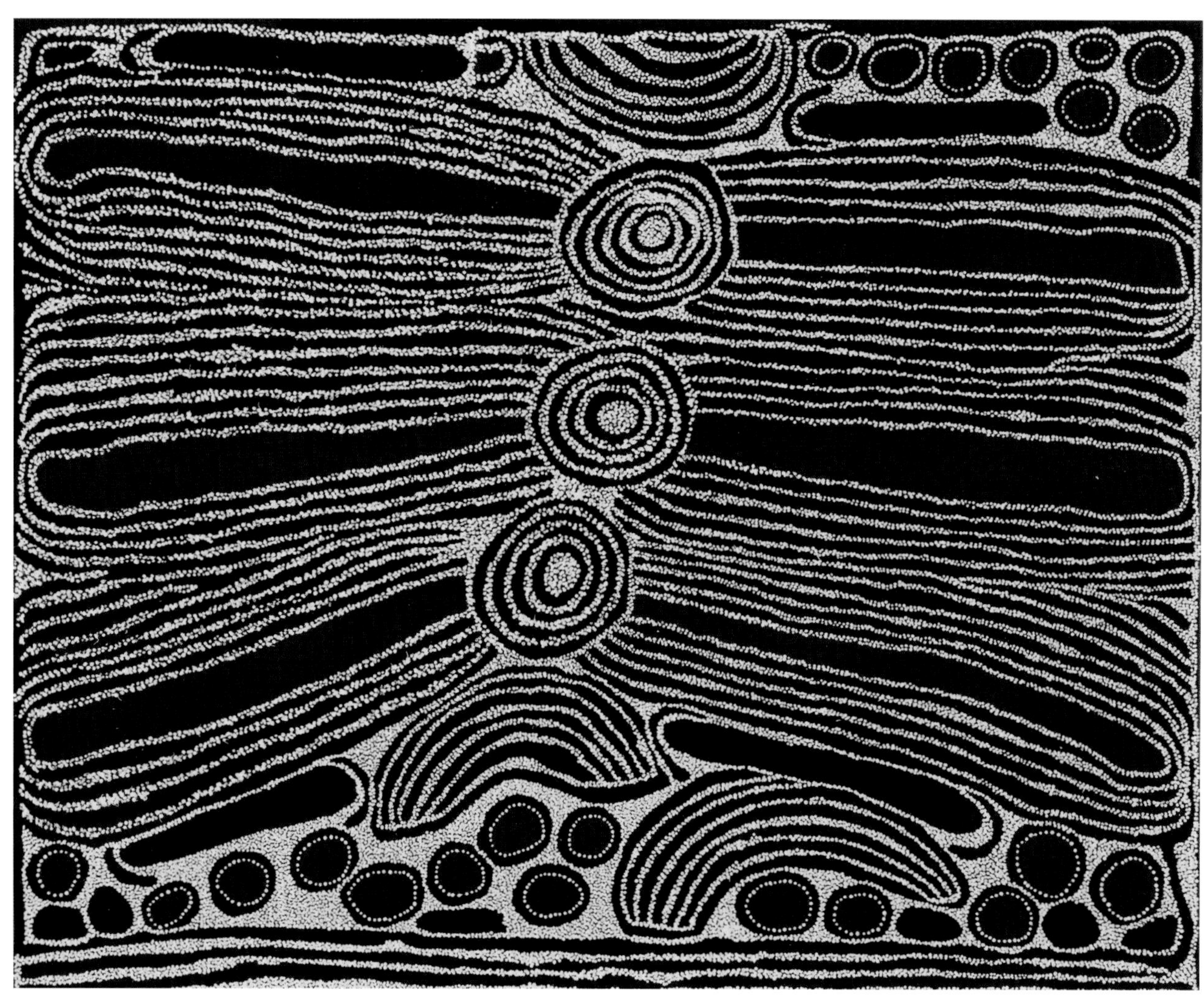

Ningura Napurrula, *Untitled* 2012, acrylic on Belgian linen, 151 x 183 cm

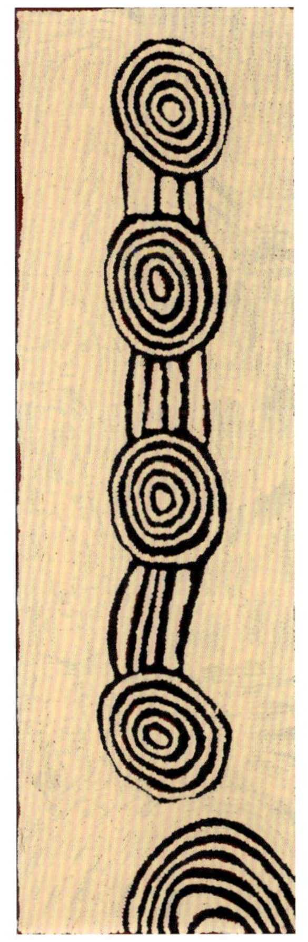

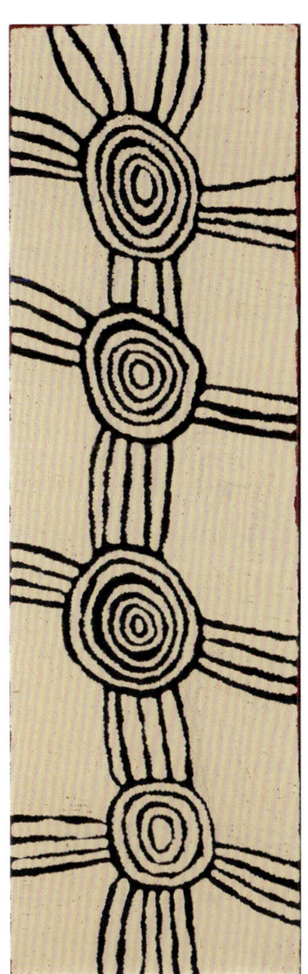

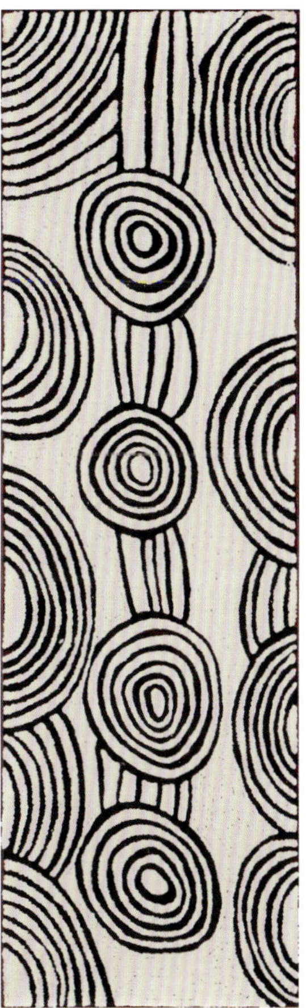

Kayi Kayi Nampitjinpa, *Untitled* 2012, acrylic on Belgian linen, 151 x 46 cm each

Ningura Napurrula, *Untitled* 2012, acrylic on Belgian linen, 150 x 150 cm

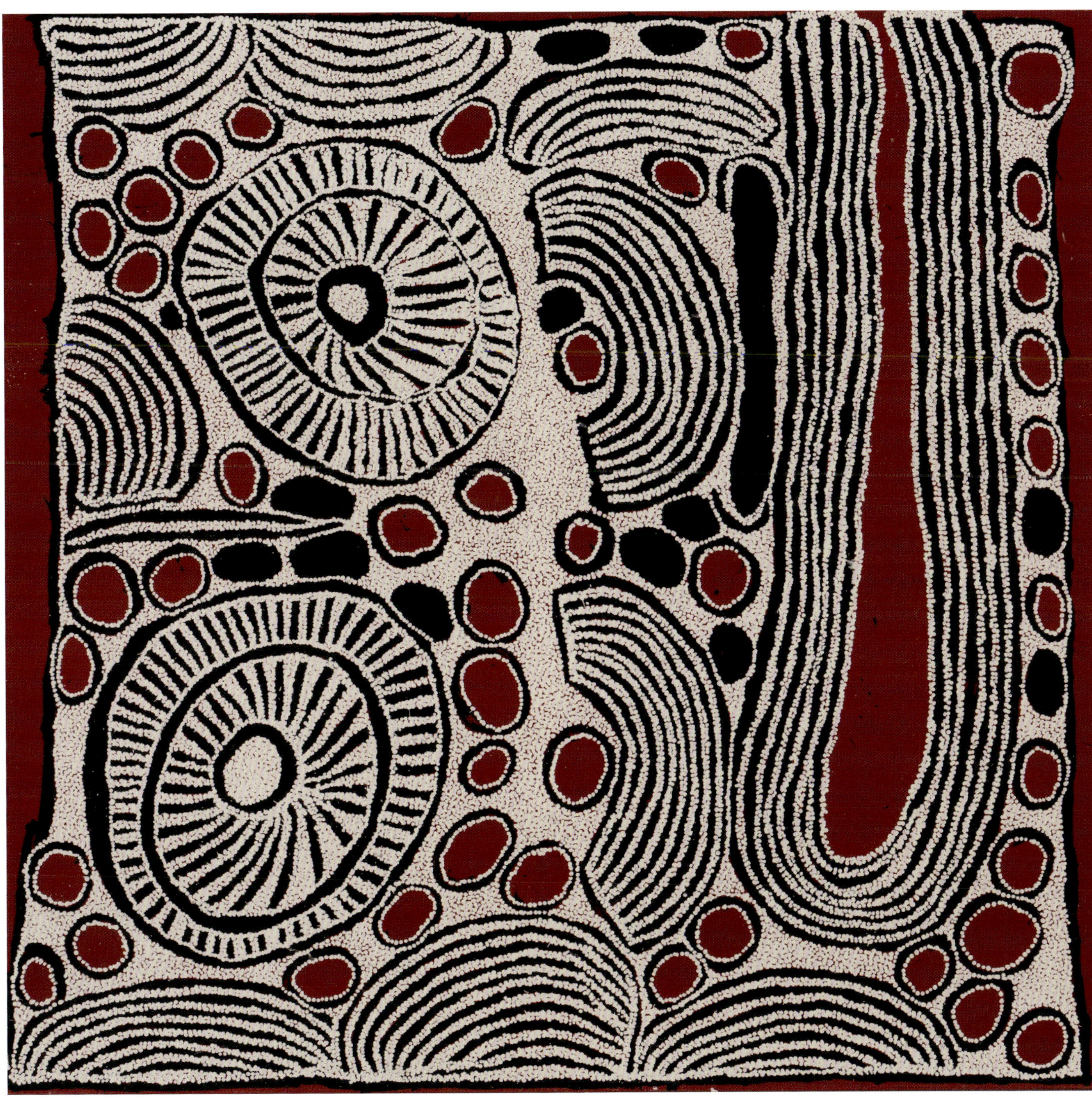

Yannima Pikarli Tommy Watson, *Untitled* 2014, acrylic on Belgian linen, 151 x 244 cm

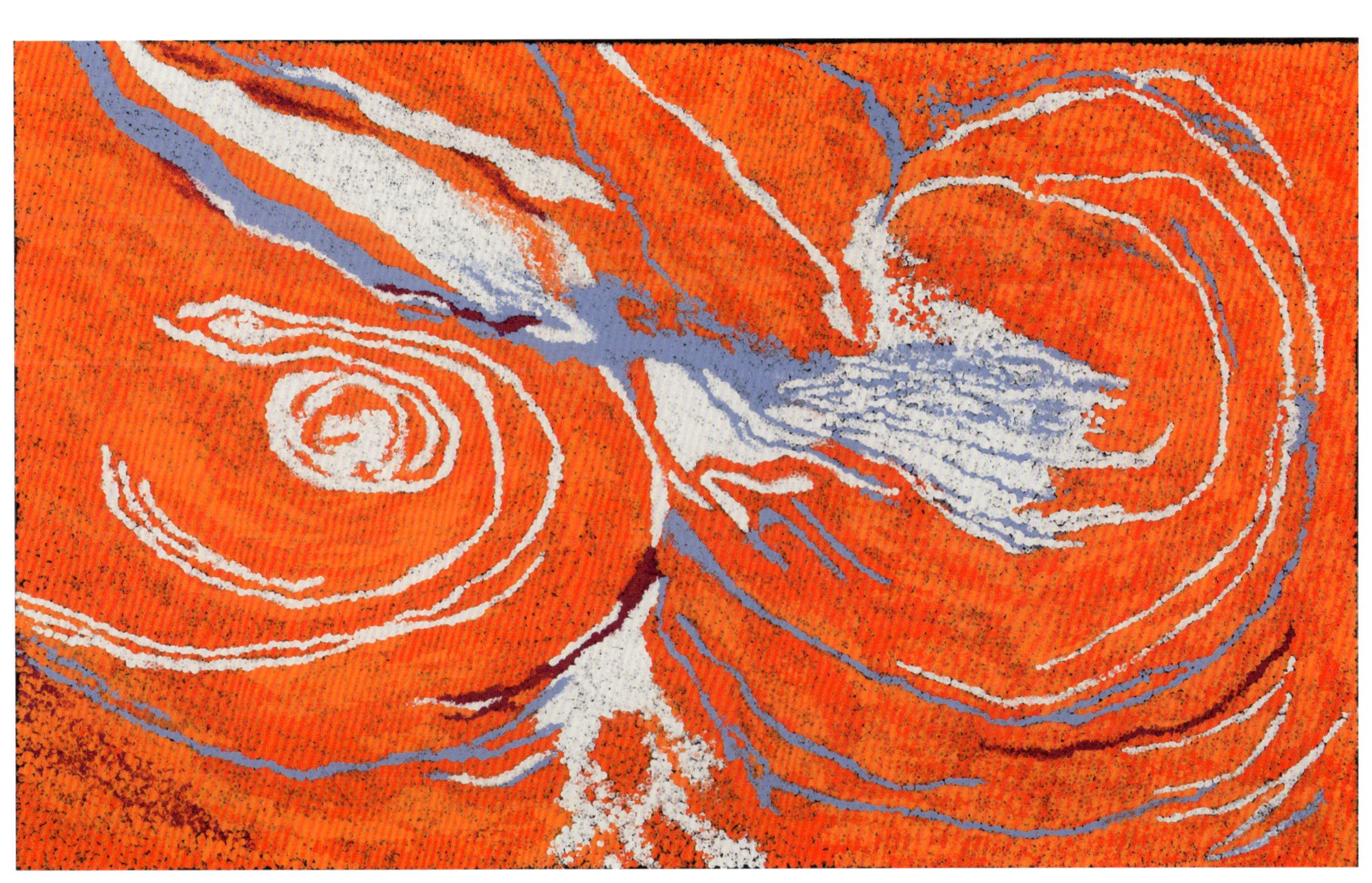

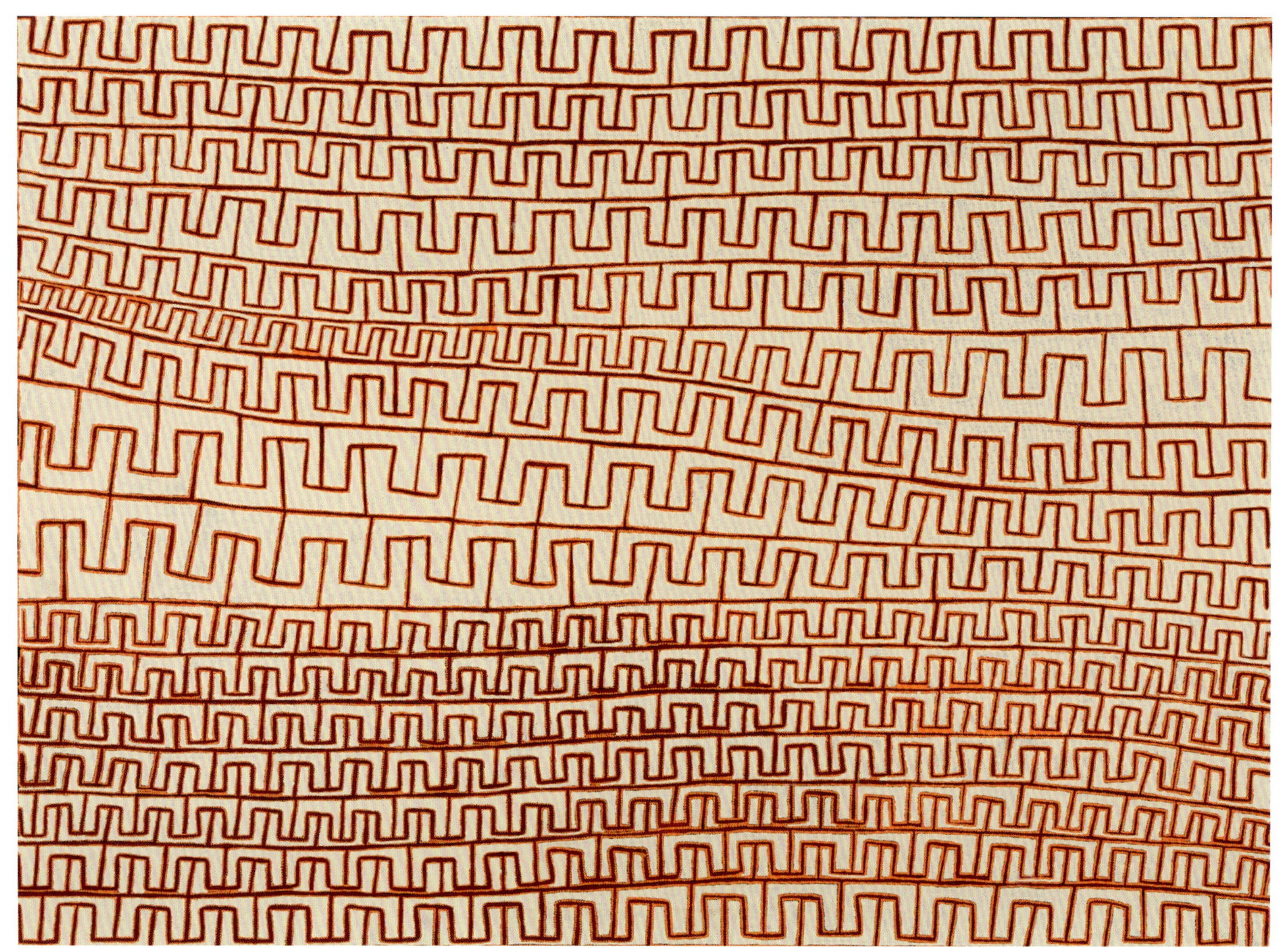

Ray James Tjangala, *Untitled* 2014, acrylic on Belgian linen, 183 x 244 cm

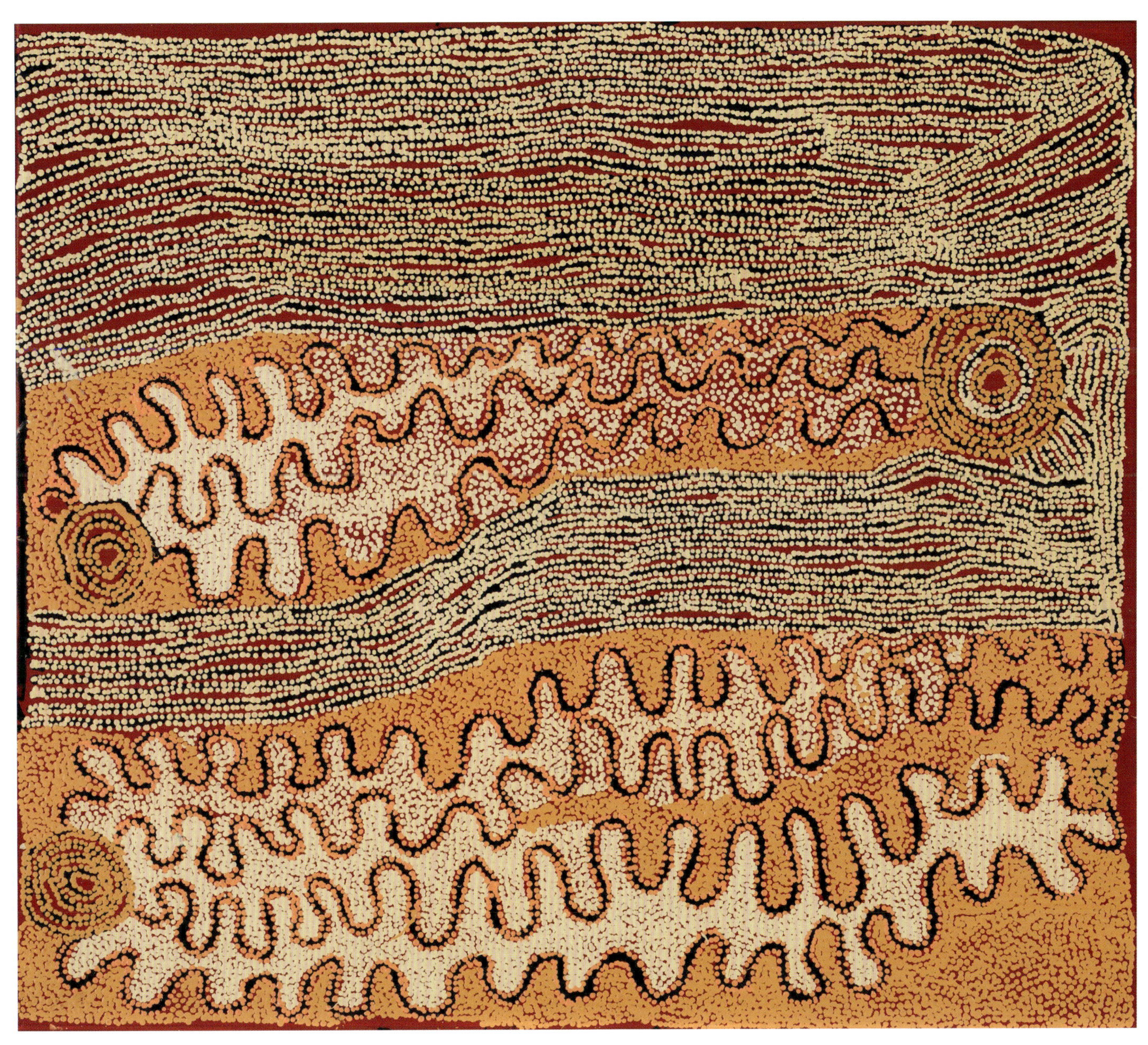

Esther Giles Nampitjinpa, *Untitled* 2013, acrylic on Belgian linen, 102 x 112 cm

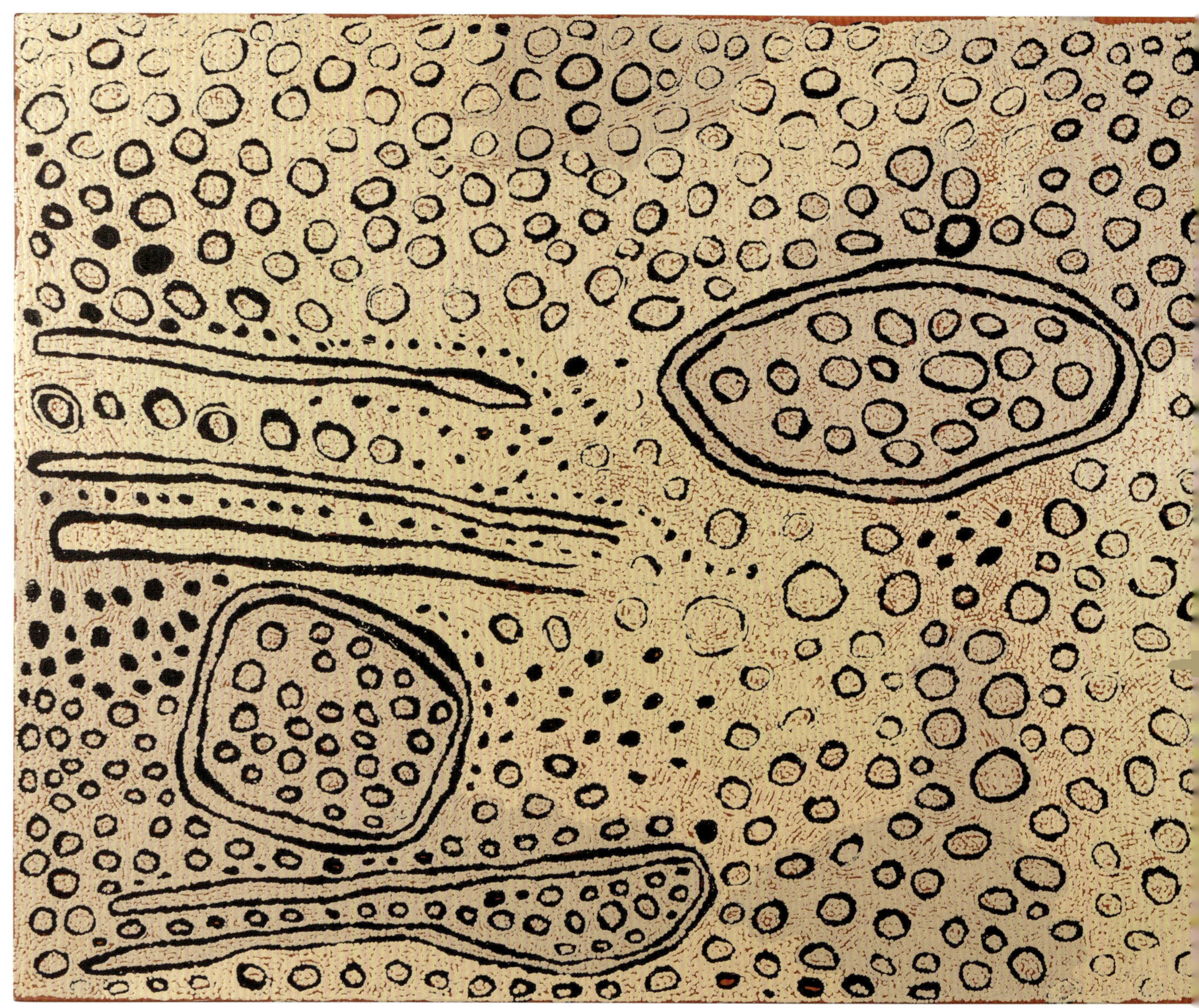

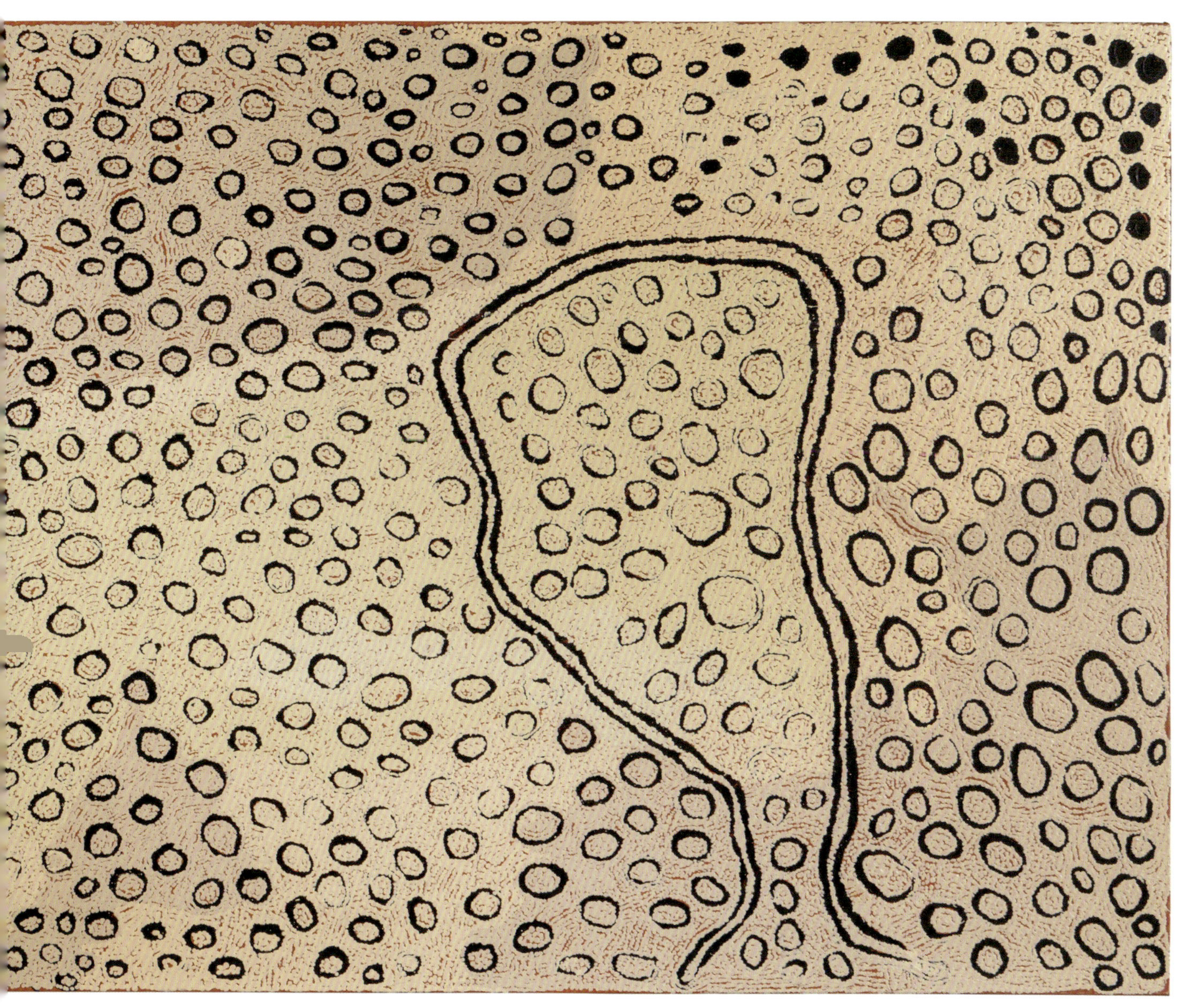

Nyurapayia Nampitjinpa (Mrs Bennett), *Punkilpirri* 2006, acrylic on Belgian linen, 122 x 305 cm

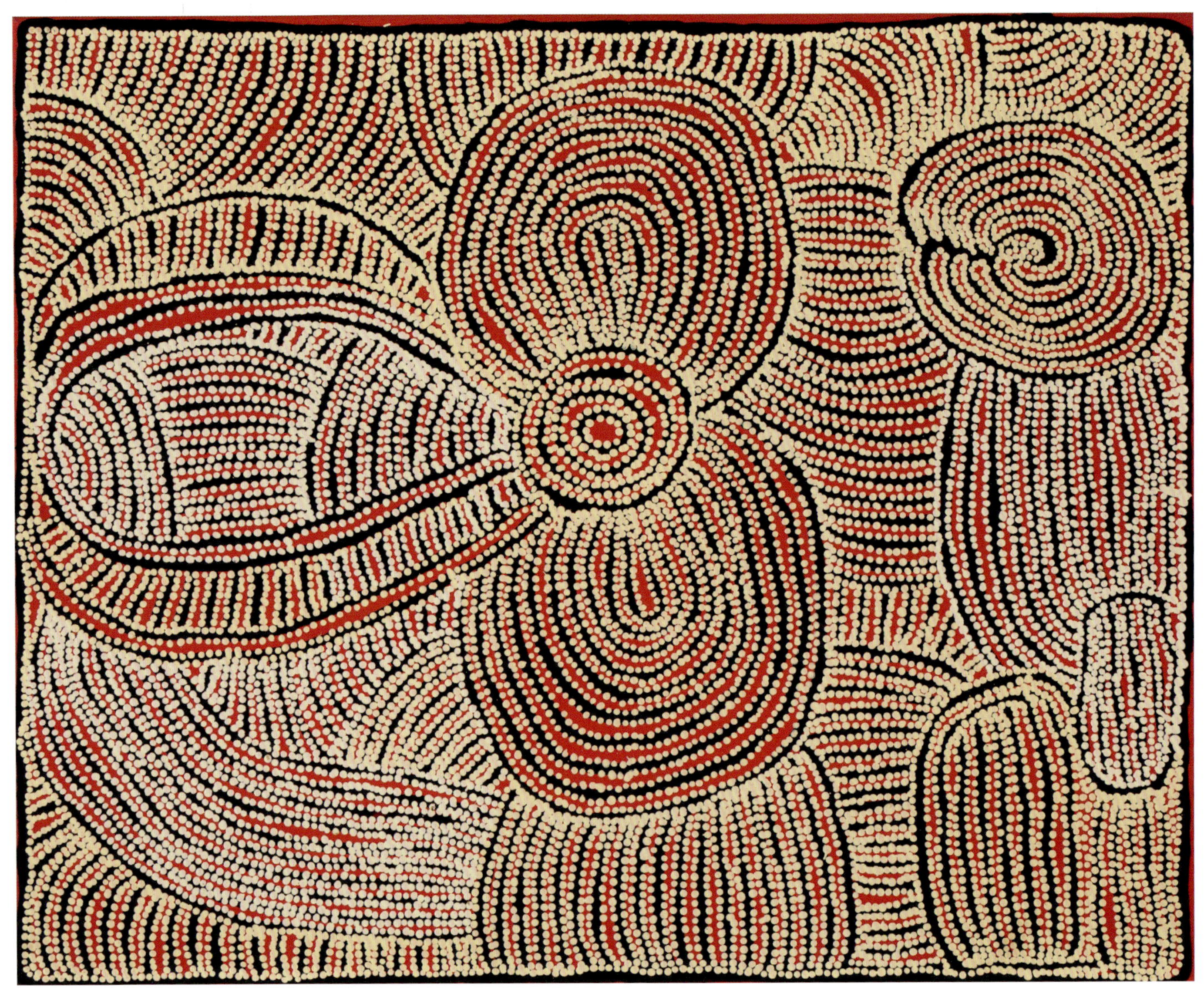

Tjawina Porter Nampitjinpa, *Untitled* 2013, acrylic on Belgian linen, 76 x 91 cm

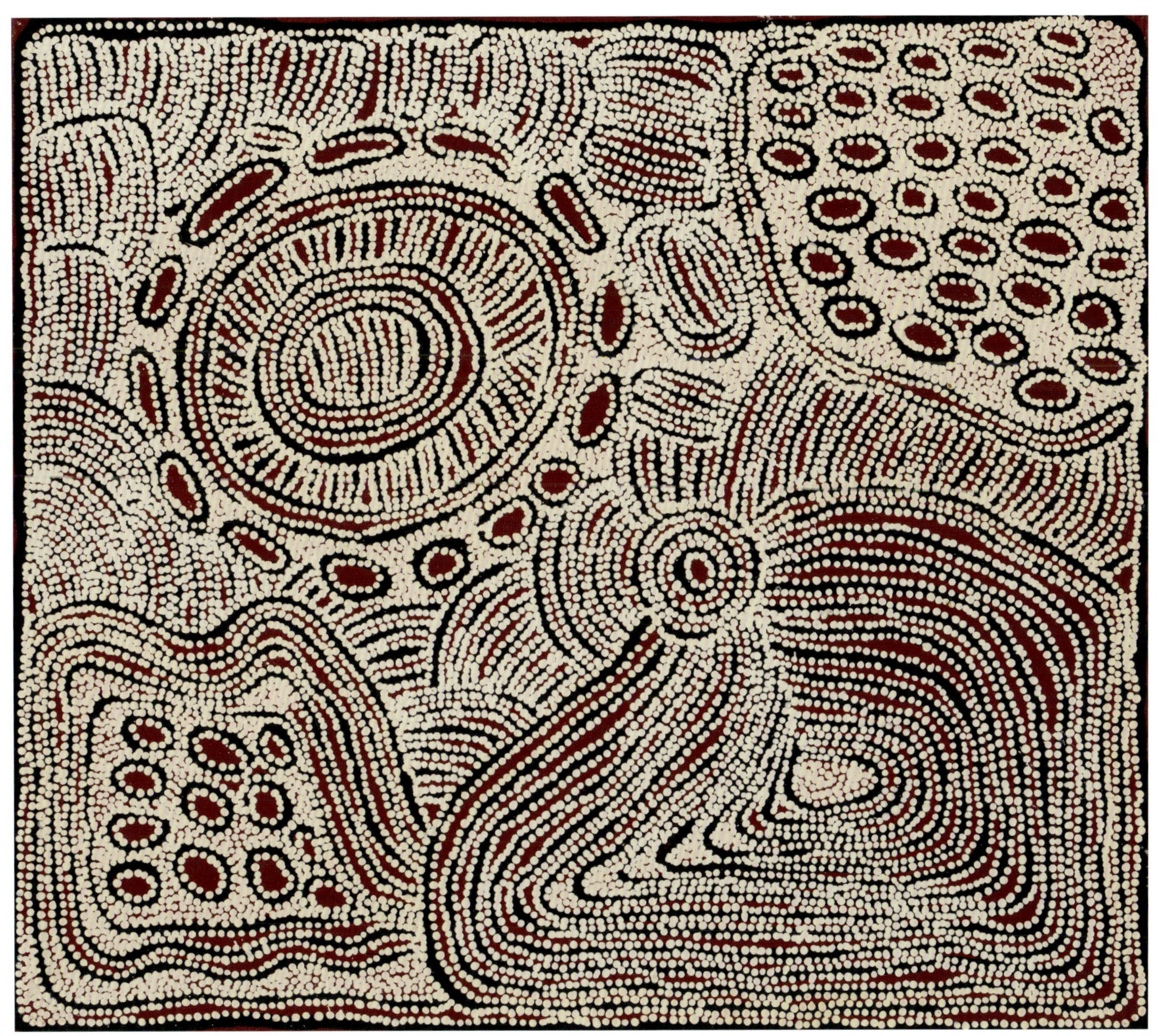

Tjawina Porter Nampitjinpa, *Untitled* 2013, acrylic on Belgian linen, 84 x 76 cm

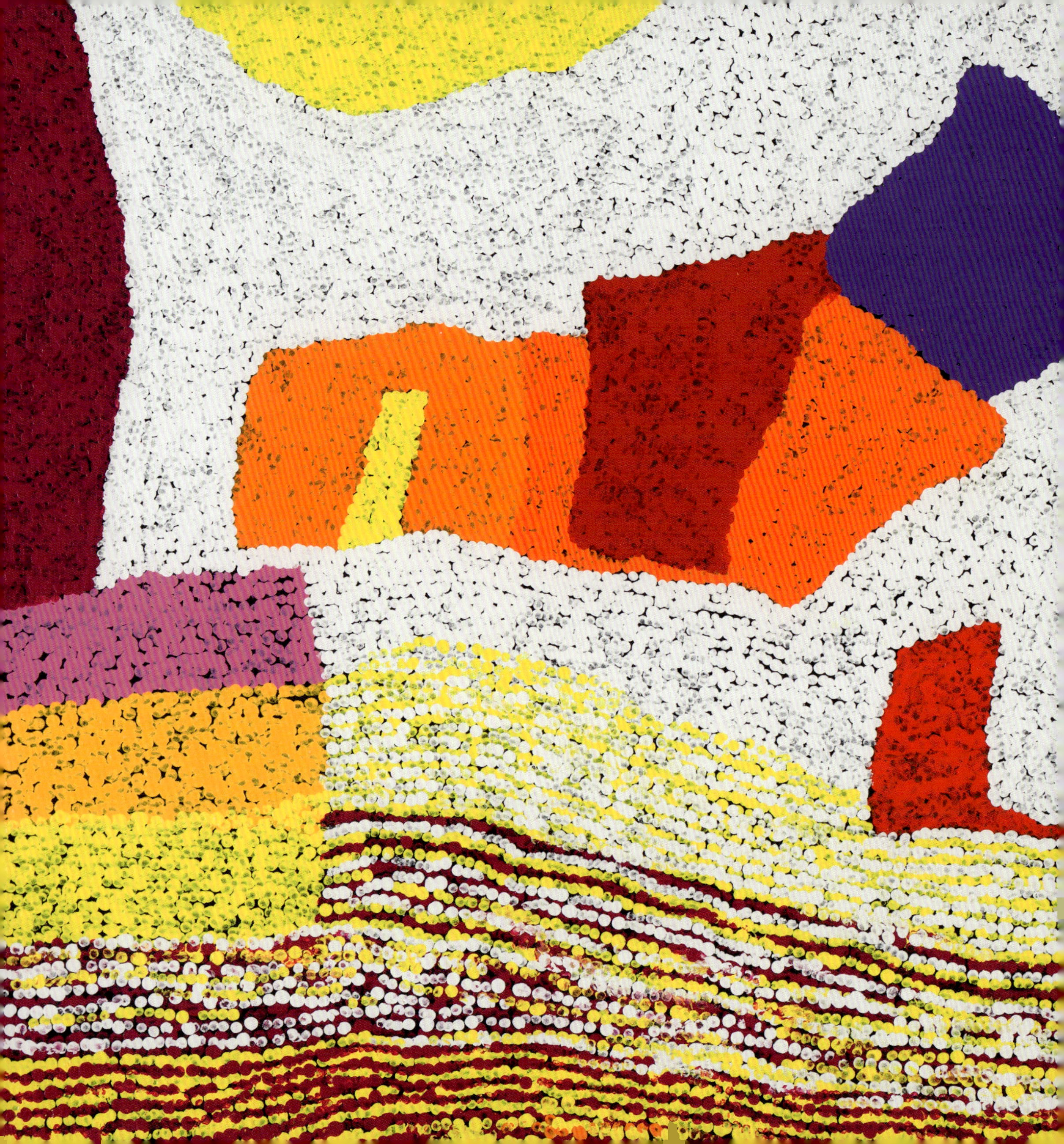

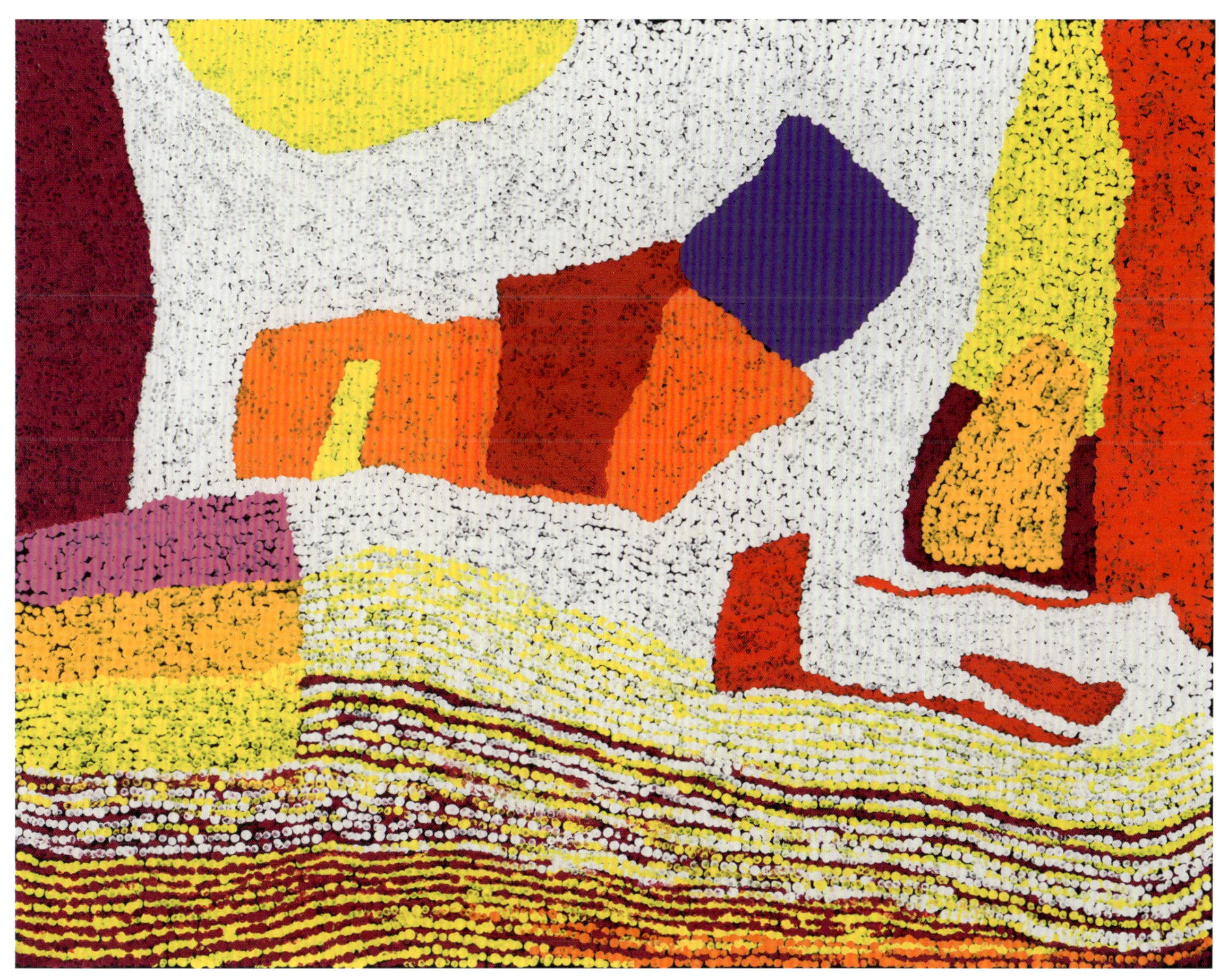

Yannima Pikarli Tommy Watson, *Untitled* 2016, acrylic on Belgian linen, 122 x 151 cm

Yannima Pikarli Tommy Watson, *Untitled* 2016, acrylic on Belgian linen, 151 x 244 cm

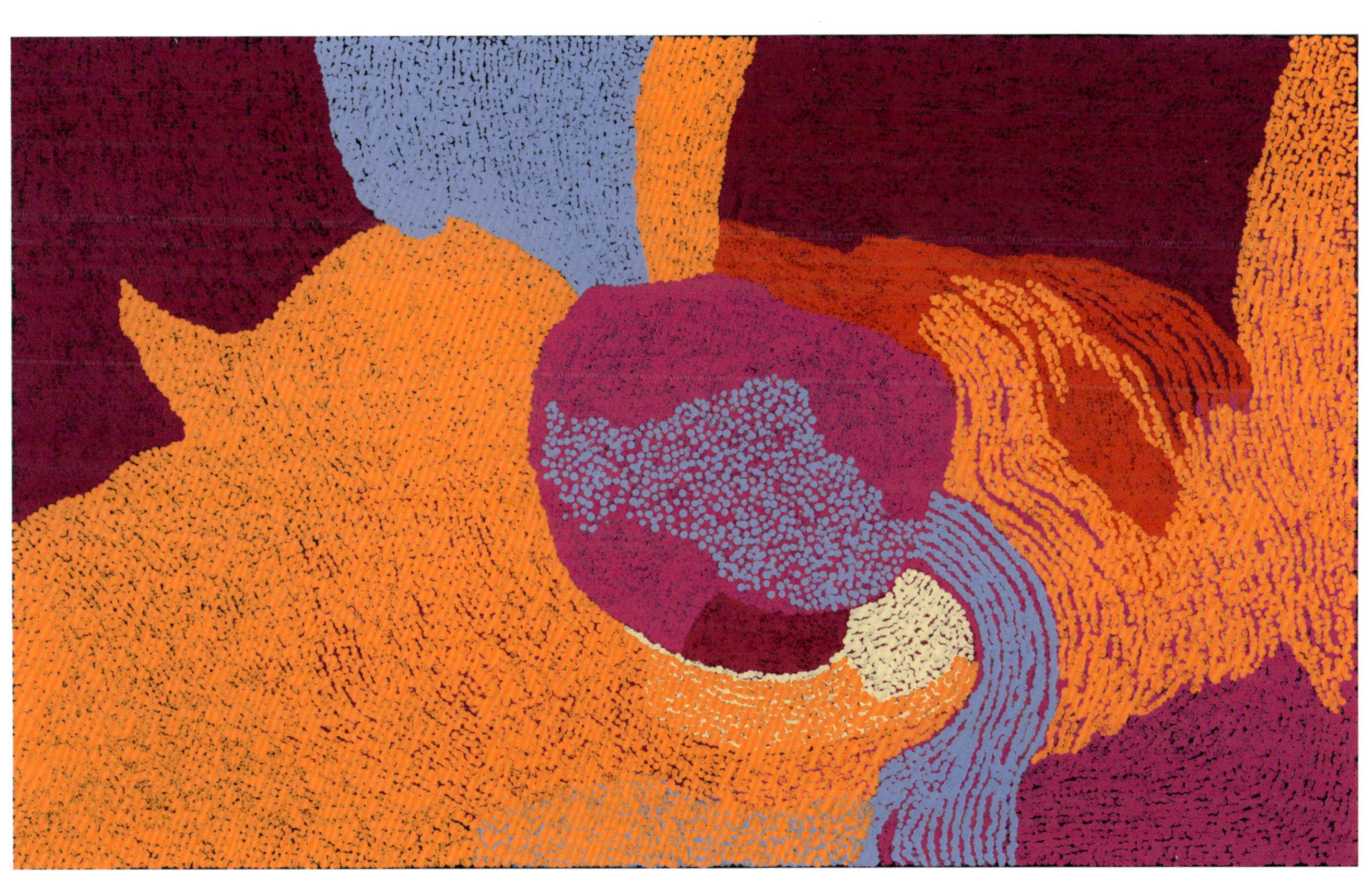

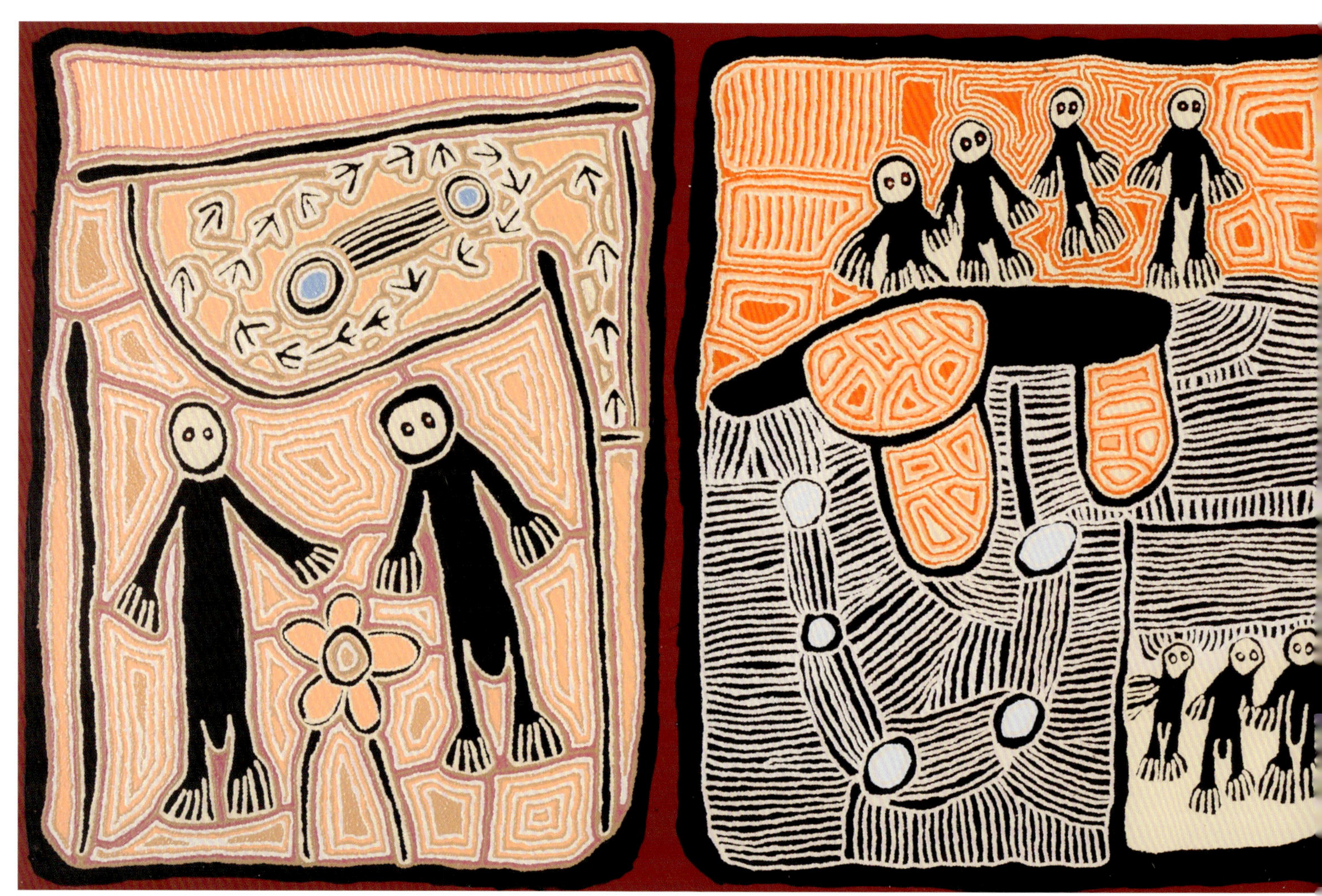

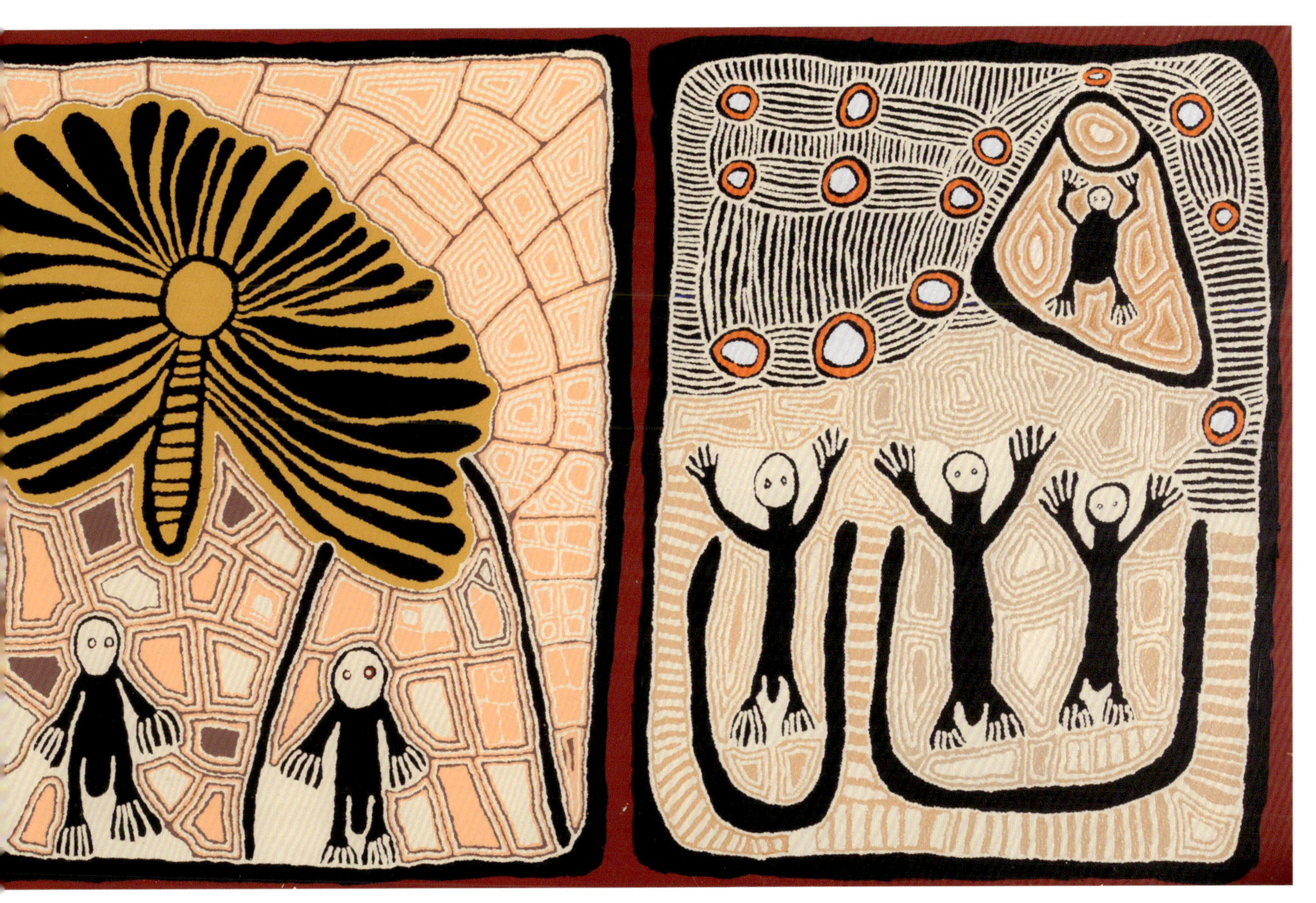

Linda Syddick Napaltjarri, *Untitled* 2013, acrylic on Belgian linen, 160 x 485 cm

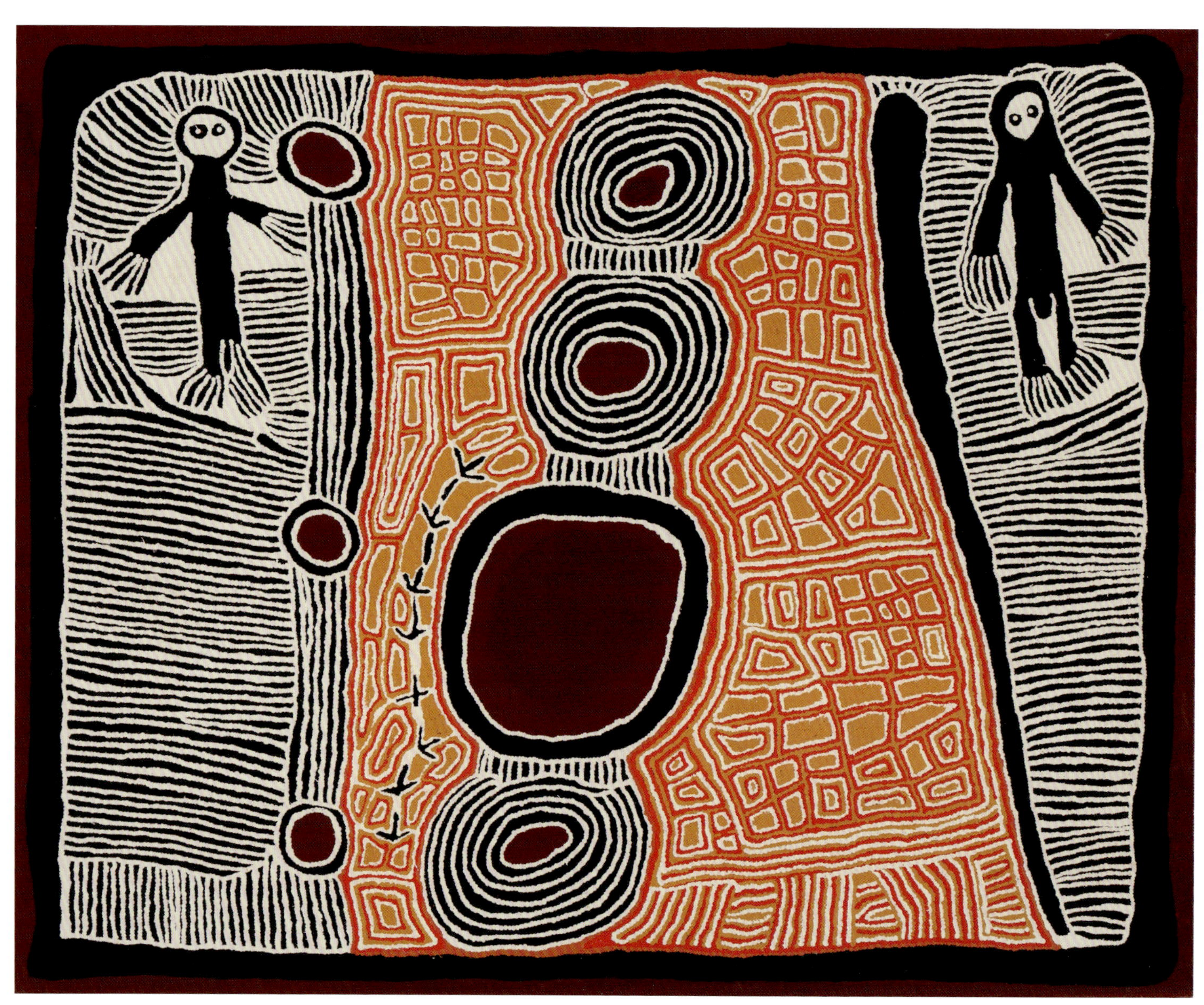

Linda Syddick Napaltjarri, *Untitled* 2013, acrylic on Belgian linen, 151 x 183 cm

## Artists in the Craig Edwards Gift

**Queenie McKenzie** – 1 work, p. 17
Born circa 1915 Mingmarriya, East Kimberley, died 1998.
Language: Gija.

**Yinarupa Gibson Nangala** – 1 work
Born circa 1955 near Jigalong, Western Australia.
Language: Pintupi.

**Esther Giles Nampitjinpa** – 11 works, pp. 53, 54, 71
Born 1948 Mirtungkatja, Western Australia.
Languages: Ngaatjatjarra and Pintupi / Luritja.

**Kayi Kayi Nampitjinpa (Barbara Reid Napangarti)** – 8 works, p. 47
Born circa 1946 Tjukurla Region, Western Australia.
Language: Ngaatjatjarra.

**Nyurapayia Nampitjinpa (Mrs Bennett)** – 3 works, p. 26
Born 1935 Mirtungkatja / Yumarra, Western Australia, died 2013.
Languages: Pitjantjatjara, Ngaatjatjarra and Pintupi.

**Tjawina Porter Nampitjinpa** – 14 works, pp. 14, 56, 57, 68, back cover
Born circa 1940 Yumarra, Western Australia.
Language: Ngaatjatjarra.

**Linda Syddick Napaltjarri** – 2 works, pp. 63, 64
Born circa 1937 Wilkinkarra (Lake Mackay), Western Australia.
Languages: Pintupi and Pitjantjatjara.

**Lorna Napanangka** – 2 works, p. 4
Born circa 1961 Haast Bluff, Northern Territory.
Language: Pintupi.

**Dorothy Napangardi** – 1 work, p. 18
Born circa 1950 Wilkinkarra (Lake Mackay), Western Australia, died 2013.
Language: Warlpiri.

**Nyungawarra Ward Napurrula** – 1 work, p. 25
Born circa 1956 Karrku, Western Australia.
Language: Ngaatjatjarra.

**Ningura Napurrula** – 5 works, pp. 46, 49
Born circa 1938 Kiwirrkurra, Western Australia, died 2013.
Language: Pintupi.

**Jorna Newberry** – 2 works
Born 1959 Angus Downs, Northern Territory.
Language: Pitjantjatjara.

**Mel Yamba Nungurrayi –** 1 work
Born circa 1957 place unknown
Language: Pintupi.

**Naata Nungurrayi** – 34 works, pp. 8, 10, 43, 44, 45, inside front cover
Born circa 1932 Kumil, Pollock Hills, Western Australia.
Language: Pintupi.

**Nancy Ross Nungurrayi** – 1 work
Born circa 1935 Maya, Northern Territory, died 2009.
Language: Pintupi.

**Tiger Palpatja** – 1 work, p. 39
Born circa 1920 Piltati, near Nyapari, South Australia, died 2012.
Language: Pitjantjatjara.

**Ray James Tjangala** – 2 works, p. 52
Born circa 1958 Yunala, near Kiwirrkura, Western Australia.
Language: Pintupi.

**Warlimpirrnga Tjapaltjarri** – 3 works, pp. 3, 20
Born circa 1958 Wilkinkarra (Lake Mackay), Western Australia.
Language: Pintupi.

**Pinta Pinta Tjapanangka** – 1 work
Born circa 1928 Yumari, Western Australia, died 1999.
Language: Pintupi.

**Wimmitji Tjapangati** – 1 work, pp. 32, front cover
Born circa 1924 Kutakurtal, Western Australia, died 1997.
Language: Kukatja.

**George Tjungurrayi** – 1 work
Born circa 1943 Kiwirrkura, Western Australia.
Language: Pintupi.

**Yannima Pikarli Tommy Watson –** 27 works, pp. 40, 51, 58, 59, 61
Born circa 1935 Anamarapiti, Western Australia.
Language: Pitjantjatjara.

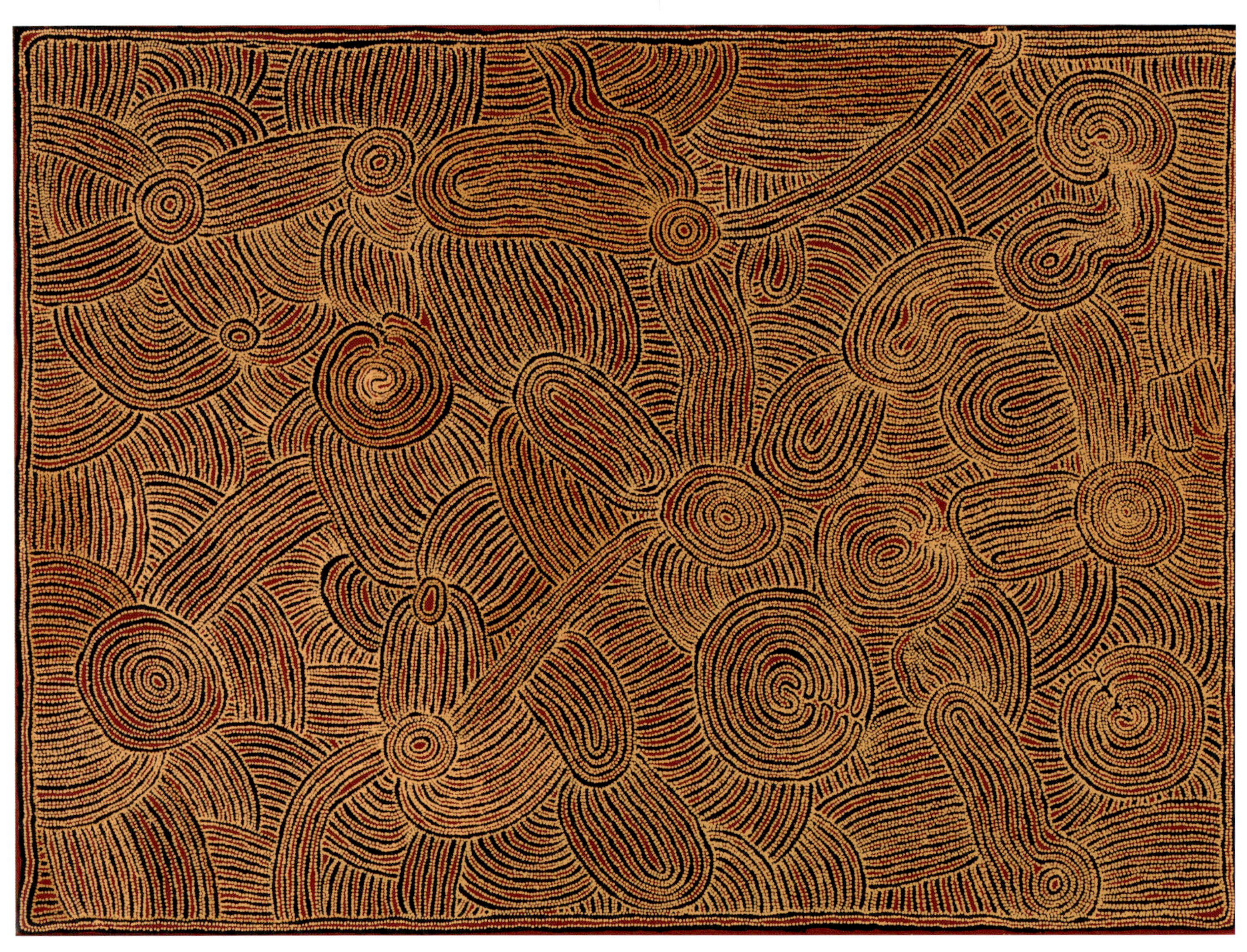

Tjawina Porter Nampitjinpa, *Untitled* 2012, acrylic on canvas, 183 x 244 cm

## Acknowledgements

With this publication and its associated exhibition we celebrate the magnificent gesture of Craig and Eve Edwards and their children Lachlan, Alexandra and Alanna in making an unprecedented gift of 120 paintings to the Australian National University art collection.

We would also like to convey our gratitude and respect to the 22 artists featured in the Edwards Collection, and to their families and communities.

For organising the conveyance of the Edwards collection to ANU and preparing works for exhibition we received indispensable help from Chris Simon at Yanda Art; Ingrid Button and Jason Barnett at IAS Fine Art Logistics; the independent art conservator Karen Holloway; Mike Welch at Hang Ups in Fyshwick; and Henry Han of The Framing Business in Canberra.

Many colleagues at ANU participated in this project – among them, Vice-Chancellor Professor Brian Schmidt; Anne Martin, Director of the Tjabal Indigenous Higher Education Centre; Associate Professor Asmi Wood; Deputy Vice-Chancellor Professor Marnie Hughes-Warrington; Chief Operating Officer Christopher Grange; the team in ANU Advancement – particularly Gwen Horsfield, Norm Bradshaw, Barbara Miles and Bianca Brownlow.

Over the past five years Craig Edwards' law firm, Maliganis Edwards Johnson, has provided financial support to the ANU Drill Hall Gallery. We thank MEJ for their continuing commitment in assisting our exhibition program, and also acknowledge the unfailing helpfulness of Craig Edwards' personal assistant, Tracey Brew.

For their contributions to this publication, our heartfelt thanks to Ian McLean for his magisterial essay, to Brian Schmidt, Anne Martin and to photographers Stephen Oxenbury and Rob Little.

This publication was designed by Tony Oates, whose help and support in other aspects of planning and organisation was invaluable too. The Curator of the ANU Art Collection, David Boon and Assistant Curator Oscar Capezio have key roles to play, and they have already begun the large task of documenting and distributing works from the Edwards Collection through the campus.

Last but not least, we acknowledge Kim Chapman, President of the Friends of the Drill Hall Gallery, who has been part of discussions ever since Craig Edwards first mooted the idea of donating some artworks to the ANU.

Terence Maloon

Director
Drill Hall Gallery & University Art Collection
Australian National University

Esther Giles Nampitjinpa, *Untitled* 2013, acrylic on Belgian linen, 84 x 76 cm

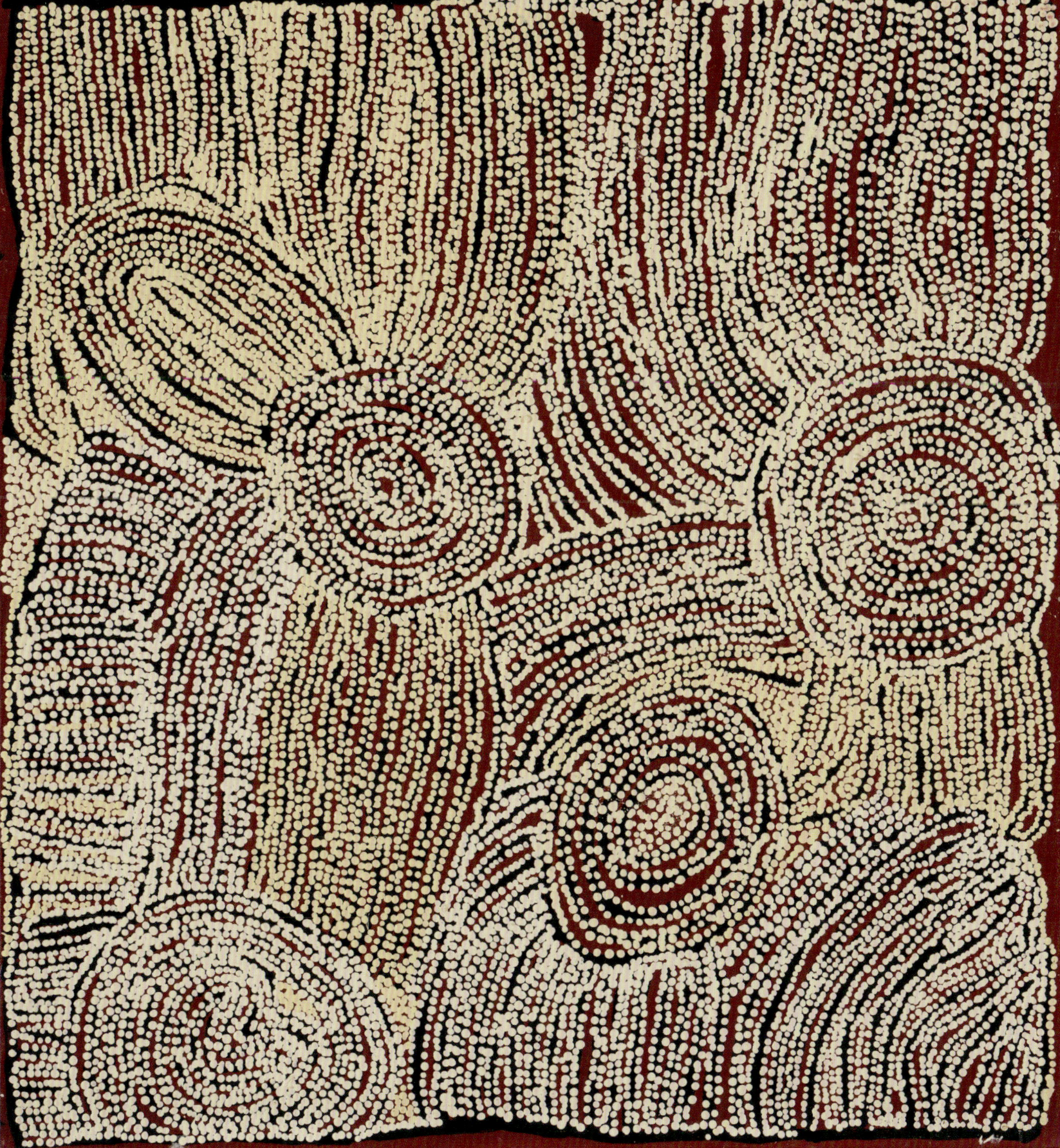

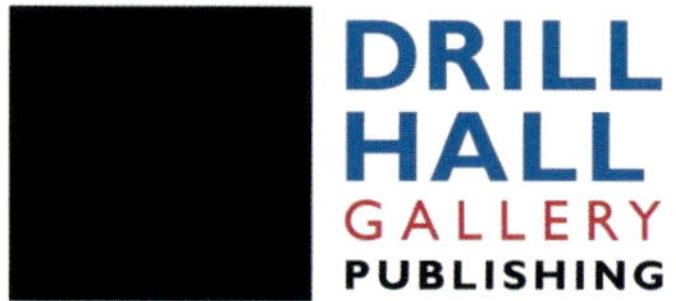


**WESTERN DESERT SUBLIME**
**The Craig Edwards Gift to the ANU**

19 October - 16 December 2018



ISBN: 978-0-9954258-8-0

Published: October 2018
Text: Anne Martin, Ian McLean, Brian Schmidt
Editor: Terence Maloon
Catalogue design: Anthony Oates
Photography: Rob Little, Stephen Oxenbury
front cover: Wimmitji Tjapangati, *Yirriwalli* 1989, acrylic on Belgian linen, 89 x 120 cm
inside cover: Naata Nungurrayi, *Iconography* 2008, acrylic on Belgian linen, 183 x 244 cm
inside back cover: Tjawina Porter Nampitjinpa, *Untitled* 2012, acrylic on canvas, 183 x 244 cm

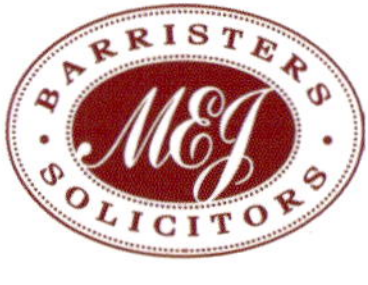


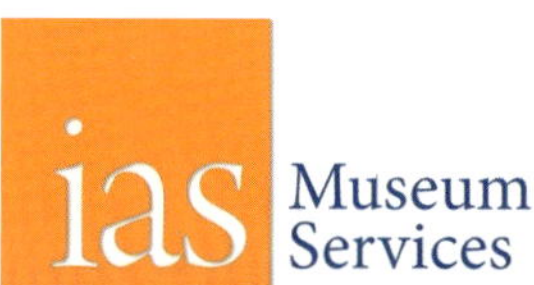


Director: Terence Maloon
Curator, Exhibitions: Tony Oates
Curator, Collection: David Boon
Manager, Outreach: Jeanette Brand
+ 61 2 6125 5832 dhg@anu.edu.au
dhg.anu.edu.au

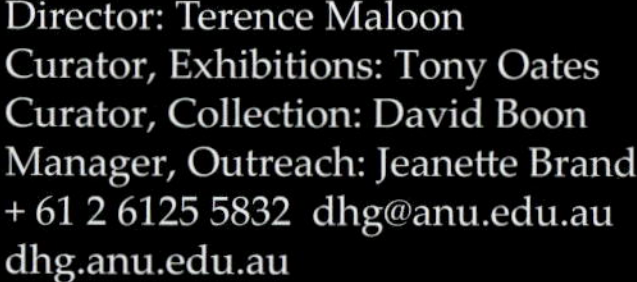

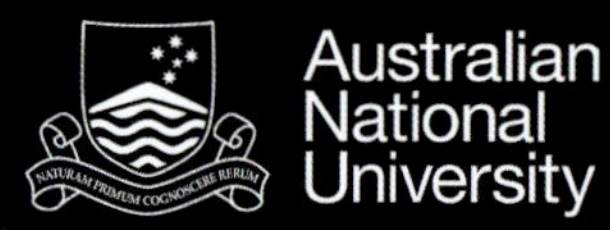